The Legend of
Satan's Bullpen
A Fantasy Baseball Fantasy

ISBN: 978-0-578-62004-6

Intro

This is the story of a very real fantasy baseball league, with very real owners. Most of this Legend is true, but as with any legend, the events have been embellished. Now into its second decade, Satan's Bullpen was intended to be a place where fantasy baseball mastery was rewarded, where ambition triumphed over negligence, and where fair rules were voted on and enforced. Over the years, those intentions were carried out under the watchful eye of the Brown Mosquito. The league developed, evolved. And then something happened. A galaxy that was always there became visible.

Owners came and went, but the core remained. Many of the characters in this story are still in the League. Some underwent metamorphic changes, like Cali Green, who physically transformed himself into a Hallucinating Hummingbird. But that is a story for another day. This is a historical anthology, and therefore, an official League document.

Within these pages, the Brown Mosquito recounts the miraculous and most outrageous climb to glory in the history of fantasy sports. This is a tale of a group of young, delinquent bartenders who started a fantasy baseball league that would change the world forever.

To begin, the name Satan's Bullpen was not chosen by the members of the league but mystically anointed upon them, a reminder that the Devil himself controlled the fantasy universe at the time, and like a flame-throwing reliever warming up in the bullpen, these rebellious owners would be called upon late in the game.

The events and the people represented in this account are both factual and invented. Easily offended readers should be warned, this crass history of the universe of fantasy baseball is boorish, tasteless, and at times truly disgusting. If a non-fictional character in the story is insulted or made to feel uncomfortable, this was most likely intended. The Brown Mosquito has a venomous stinger and he is not afraid to use it. He's had to fight for everything he's ever had. His journey to the peak of immortality was remarkable, as was the path of all of the others in the League. Spit from the ass of Satan himself, the Brown Mosquito was somehow able to bring this band of misfits together and lead them to fantasy greatness.

In a time when fantasy baseball needed them most, these ten owners banded together and fought the destructive forces of evil side by side.

It was in their blood to fight. And in their hearts not to fail.

This is the Legend of Satan's Bullpen.

Final Regular Season Standings
Satan's Bullpen
2009

1. Brown Mosquitos	17 - 5
2. Crazy Fool	14 - 8
3. Mesa T's	13 - 9
4. SB Cherry Poppers	12 - 10
5. Newport Idiots	11 - 11
6. Happy HairyBalls	11 - 11
7. San Francisco Tranny's On Crak	10 - 12
8. Cali Green	9 - 13
9. Captain Shitbeard	7 - 15
10. Team Rosebudd	6 - 16

The Legend of the Brown Mosquito

Back in the dawn of time, in the age before Satan's Bullpen, the fantasy world was a lost and dangerous place. Chaos ran amok. Pollution and dark skies had encroached on what used to be a pleasurable past-time. The baseball era had entered a period of evil and greed. A powerful leader rose among the savage and blood-thirsty. His arms were super-human, his powerful legs crushed everything underneath when he walked the scorched earth. With a large blistering red head filled with fury and craze, this demon captured his power when he defeated Sammy Sosa in the Battle of the Bats. He became America's hero, the man who broke Roger Maris. He ruled over baseball with his henchmen Barry Bonds and Alex Rodriguez and bombarded the fantasy universe with artificial home runs, synthetic muscle mass, ass-juiced table squirts, and vials of steroids that were placed up Roger Clemens' butt for safekeeping.

They called him Satan, but no one really knew if this monster was the actual devil in human form, or if it was just another of his nicknames, like Big Red, or Big Mac. He was originally known as Mark McGwire, but that name had long left him. The imposing red-faced beast smashed all the records, took whatever he wanted, and soon there was nothing left. All the integrity and passion for fantasy baseball dissipated until it was nearly extinct, and all the interest went into other sports of wager. Fantasy Football. Fantasy Basketball. Fan Duel. Masters pools. College Football Bowl Game Pools. Home Run Derby Pools. Celtics-Lakers Mat Shots. March Madness.

Fantasy baseball was left for dead, devoured by the ruthless and unnaturally strong clan. Big Mac was at the center of it all, soaking in all the power. His greed was insatiable, without the slightest hint of shame or remorse.

Like a frightened girl, fantasy baseball hid, in gutters and in sewers, in swamps and bogs and garbage-filled rivers of jizz. Meanwhile, the players continued to grow in size. Baseballs exploded out of ballparks. Records continued to fall. And still, fantasy baseball ducked and dodged and dove into mountains of shit and said: “It's nice in here.” Ryan

Braun said "I wanna hit 40 home runs. Give me some of that juice." There seemed no way out of this Hell.

Well, time went on, and McGwire got lazy. His juicy ass sat on his riches and records, his blood pressure reduced to a simmer, his face relaxed to a bright pink, and he even had the audacity to become a hitting coach in the majors.

One day, as he watched his players take batting practice from the dugout, there was a rumbling in his stomach. A gas-infused pain deep in his bowels. He shifted uncomfortably in his too-tight white Cardinals uniform as the pain grew to an uncomfortable level. He tried to remain focused on the field, tried not to look Tony LaRussa in the eye, but something was seriously wrong.

The players covered their ears as a deafeningly high-pitched squeal — long and drawn out — pierced the air like a dog whistle, and then a hypodermic needle with wings was violently ejected from the butt of Mark McGwire.

The flying needle bzzzzzzzzzz'd around the dugout, it's body a vile of blood and steroids, it's thin pointed nose and sharp wings buzzing inches from players' waving arms and sensitive ears. Panic ensued. Bzzzzzzzzzzzzzzzz. BzzzzzzzzZZZZzzzz. BzZZZzzzzzZZZZZzzzzzzz. Buckets of bubble gum were knocked over, sunflower seeds spilled into the air, arms waved, legs flailed as the Brown Mosquito buzzed around aimlessly, drunk on the sauce of Big Mac's ass.

The Mosquito eventually found sunlight and flew out and over the ball field, his large bug eyes witnessing the beautiful sights of the diamond-shaped infield, the freshly mowed outfield grass, the cotton-candy clouds on a brilliant blue sky over Busch Stadium in St. Louis. Lines pure, straight and white. Tall yellow foul poles. Players in symmetrical positions on a field of perfect dimensions. A ball was thrown. SNAP. A glove made the catch. The air smelled like popcorn and the breeze carried the Brown Mosquito to the wall along the right field foul line.

From that fence, he watched the players and learned the game of fantasy baseball. He knew immediately he could do this better. Much better. The greed and rage inherited from McGwire sparked his frenzy, and the Brown Mosquito left to start his own league. A league built on integrity, as integrity would be the only weapon to take down Satan and his henchmen.

His first stop was the Bogs of Thyne, where there lived an old hermit named TJ who supposedly dealt in mystical powers. It would be there that the Brown Mosquito would begin to craft and develop the now illustrious league known as Satan's Bullpen.

The Bogs of Thyne

Rivers of floating hot algae steaming with venom bubbled beneath a sky that never brightens. A lingering, insatiable heat persisted. Disease-carrying micro-bodies and insects hovered over big deposits of feces. The pungent smell would be intolerable to our evolved palate today, but at the time the creatures who lived in the Bogs of Thyne were adapted to it and used the strong aromas to hunt down protein in the form of vermin and rodents living in the deposits of shit from larger creatures.

The BROWN MOSQUITO guided his aircraft like an X-Wing Fighter over piles of dung and the swarms of insects. A flying cockroach WHIZZED PAST -- nearly colliding, but the Brown Mosquito flew through the orchestrated chaos with expert precision.

A sudden swarm of turd-eating-gnats PELTED the X-Wing Fighter and the Brown Mosquito struggled to hang on. Lost in a blizzard of gnats and shit, he went down, but regained control at the last instant and pulled his needle tipped nose up above the rushing river of feces and garbage. He flew on, determined, on a crucial mission to find the only one who could help him. Somewhere in a land called Tijuana.

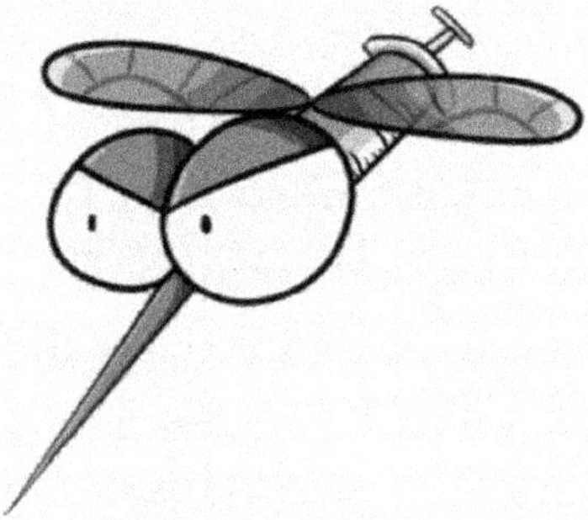

In a poor village, in the center of town, a little boy cobbled shoes. When his work was done at the shop, he walked over to the local pub to wash dishes. The town was dreary, the poor were everywhere, any sense of hope was lost long ago. The little cobbler bumped past people on his way to the pub, his head down, searching the cobblestones as he walked. Someday, he would think, he'd find a stone on that street that was any other color than grey.

The pub was its normal boisterous self, with a joyous hymn of loud music and singing, glasses clinking and jingling, some breaking and some being thrown and SMASHED against the wall. The little cobbler, TJ, walked in the back door and into the kitchen. He broke off a piece of bread and quickly ate it, his only meal of the day. He went to the sink and observed the mountain of dishes piled high and sighed.

At the bar, CAPTAIN SHITBEARD was pouring Mai-Tai's as fast as he could, sliding them across the bar and tossing money into a bucket. The Captain had a beard of shit, and little pieces of leftover bread and grease and meat dangled from it. The crowd inside grew louder and Shitbeard tried to keep up, dancing around the bar with the grace of a very drunk ballerina.

The Brown Mosquito flew in through the open harbor window on a waft of seafood-smelling sea breeze and buzzed around the crowd. A bunch of hammerheads were all getting angry fighting to get to the bar. The Mosquito saw that the Captain was struggling to keep up, so he burst into action. He buzzed behind the bar, started doing dishes like a machine, then wiped the bar down, flipped napkins in front of all the guests, and had drinks in their hands before the Captain had even looked up.

The Brown Mosquito bzzzzzZZZZzzzzZZZzzzzz'd across Captain Shitbeard's face. He swatted and cursed and spit and cursed some more but the Brown Mosquito was too quick. The Mosquito quickly made 12 "Nora the Explorer" races with 2 straws each and slide them to everyone at the bar.

The whole placed CHEERED!

The little boy came out from the kitchen to see what was going on as drinks were being served at an impossible pace. Money started piling up and around the tip bucket as it reached its full capacity and started spilling all across the back bar. TJ had never seen anything like it. The patrons were happy and singing and drunkenly hugging and laughing and slapping each other on the back.

Captain Shitbeard couldn't believe it. He was known as the greatest bartender in Thyne Bog Harbor, but the Brown Mosquito's skills were unquestionable. He offered him half the money, and a lifetime partnership of friendship and Bill Cosby impressions.

Despite the Captain being a well-known back-stabbing pirate, the Brown Mosquito accepted the offer and was introduced to TJ, his bar-back.

"You?" The Brown Mosquito was dumbfounded. "You are the one they call TJ?"

He had heard stories of TJ being hundreds of years old, a shrunken old man – not a pudgy little boy.

The boy nodded his head.

"Well, then," said the Brown Mosquito. "This is for you."

From behind his back, he presented TJ with a baseball.

The boy had never seen anything like it. He held it in his hands. A different kind of cobblestone, he thought.

"I'd like to take you on an amazing journey," the Brown Mosquito said. "There is a whole world out there for you to see. And it all revolves around that."

TJ gazed at the baseball. Its powers were no doubt mystical.

The Mosquito noticed that Captain Shitbeard was also looking at the baseball, his eyes growing large with greed.

TJ dropped his head and handed the baseball back up to the Brown Mosquito.

"I can't go. I have to stay," he said. "I need to provide for my family." He turned and walked away back through the bar crowd.

The Brown Mosquito turned angry. He didn't fly all this way to be turned away by the hermit boy. Thinking quickly, he buzzed around the bar, filling his injector nose with Wild Turkey, Midori, and Bacardi 151 – a Bonsai Pipeline. With his tank full of green fire, he buzzed across the bar, through the shoulders and elbows of patrons and right into his target of TJ's left butt cheek. He drained the Bonsai Pipeline into TJ's bloodstream, and the boy stumbled across the floor. He crashed into the jukebox, holding onto it as the Bonsai worked its way through him.

TJ's eyes narrowed, his tongue felt alive, and he even felt it in his plums. He straightened out, zeroed in on the jukebox, and played Green Grass and High Tides Forever and burst into air guitar.

"FACE-MELTERS!!!!!!!" CALI GREEN shouted from across the room, wearing a Jimi Hendrix outfit with a bandana tied around his golden locks.

Then Cali Green jumped up on the bar and ripped the Green Grass and High Tides guitar solo on air guitar. The Brown Mosquito and Captain Shitbeard continued to race around the bar, pouring drinks and collecting money. The baseball sat on a shelf behind the bar. Its powers were growing.

The Cantina

They were an unusual crew, to say the least, and received plenty of stares as they walked up the cobblestone street; the Brown Mosquito, Captain Shitbeard, Cali Green, and TJ (dressed in a Mesa T's little league shirt, carrying a bat and a glove).

The Mosquito led the way, feasting on the blood of strangers. Captain Shitbeard navigated with his one good eye, a heavy dose of liquor running through his veins. Cali Green walked in a green haze. And Taylor Jordan skipped ahead with his glove dangling from his bat.

"You think we're gonna meet some real Major League players?" TJ could barely contain his excitement.

"It's not that kind of baseball, TJ," said the Brown Mosquito.

"Are ye going to war?!" spat the Captain.

"Yes," affirmed the Brown Mosquito.

“Well then I’m in,” said the Captain. “I’m a headin’ ta sea on me ship right now. Call ’er The Endless Summer. She sleeps in ’er slip right yonder like a baby in ’er cradle.”

He points up at a seaside restaurant.

“That’s not a ship,” said the Mosquito. “That is a restaurant.”

“No way, man! That’s not a restaurant?” Cali Green was thoroughly confused.

The Captain barked, “That is a restaurant! And a ship! Mine! And I’ll sail ’er out ta seas a’ plenty, in search of a booty of lavish treasure! In fact, some even say there's women made ’a gold out o’er the Western horizon. I’ll set a course to find the golden ladies and soon I shall be floating on a cloud of titties.”

"That restaurant is not going anywhere," said the Brown Mosquito. "What we need is a real ship."

"A real ship?" TJ's eyes were as big as saucers.

"Yes, TJ," said the Brown Mosquito, "Now shut the fuck up. You let me do all the talking in there. And you — " he grabbed Captain Shitbeard by the collar. "No fighting."

"Arggh, I do believe I'll find me'self a drink."

Inside, the cantina was bumping. Funny looking animals played funny looking instruments. The bar served cold steaming mugs of something. The Captain shoved his way in. "I'll 'ave two," he ordered the bartender. "And put two more on ice for me."

The Mosquito looked around, buzzing around the place. He was looking for someone. Cali Green, otherwise known as Sean Lappi, ambled along, tilting his shades lower and checking out the girls.

"HEY!" A loud shout froze them. An ugly doorman held TJ by the shoulder. "He can't be in here!"

"He grew up in a bar," shouted Captain Shitbeard. "He can handle himself."

"I tell ya, I don't want no pi---" the man is CRACKED across the knees with the baseball bat from TJ, crippling him immediately.

In something closely resembling a smile, the Captain said, "Told ya."

TJ put his baseball bat back on his shoulder and joined the Captain at the bar. "What are ya having TGay?"

"Vodka soda," the little guy said. He tried to climb up onto a barstool but it was too high. The Captain gave him a little boost and got him up there.

"Yah, I totally surf," Cali Green wooed a couple of ladies. "I can teach you how, ya?"

The girls giggled.

The Brown Mosquito BUZzzZED him in the ear.

"Ah! Ahh!" Cali jumped around, his flashy dance suit glittering as he shook his arms and knees. "Ahhhhh! Get it off!"

The girls giggle.

"BzzzzzzzzzZZZZZZZZzzzzzzzz!" the Mosquito buzzed in his ear.

"Ahhhh! Ok, ok! OK!"

"This is a very important mission!" yelled the Brown Mosquito. "Either you're in, or you're out."

"No, I'm in. I'm in," Cali Green forged through the crowd with a finger wiggling out the itchy ear. "How do you know what this guy looks like, man?"

"I'll know him when I see him."

And then he did. Sitting in a booth. Next to a giant hairy creature.

The Mosquito landed on the table in front of him.

"Adam Horn?" the Mosquito asked.

"Who wants to know?" Under the table, the man put his finger on the trigger of his laser-blaster.

"Someone who needs a very fast ship."

"A very fast ship? Is 12 par-secks fast enough for you?" Horn was smug, and good-looking, and he knew it. He used his charm to get out of many tight spots. "Gonna cost ya, kid."

"We can pay you, but you might be more interested where we're going," said the Brown Mosquito. "You could be paid ten-fold."

"Ten-fold? What is this some kind of trick?"

His finger tickled the trigger of the blaster under the table.

The creature next to him WARRRFFFF'd.

"Easy, easy buddy," said Horn. "You better start talking — fast — or my buddy over here will rip both your arms out."

The hairy beast WAAARRRF'd again.

"We going to the Fantasy Baseball System," said the Mosquito. "In the reaches of the ESPN galaxy."

"Ha! You're funny, kid. Now get out of here so I can make some real money," Adam Horn turned away.

"I'm telling you, we can get you your money. Ten teams, $100 entry fee. Week-to-week, head-to-head matchups."

"Head-to-Head matchups?" Horn was intrigued.

The Mosquito continued, "The playoffs and Championship run two weeks straight. $500 for the winner, plus another $300 if you win the Pennant."

"So you could possibly win $800?"

"Most rules are consistent," continued the Mosquito, "but we start 5 outfielders and have one Utility player. Pitchers will get 2 points for a strikeout, and negative 2 for an earned run."

"Interesting. What about homers?" asked Horn. "I've been thinking I got me a big power hitter right here." He slaps the creature on the shoulder.

"Which galaxy do you come from, man?" Cali Green wobbled, sipping a drink through a straw.

Horn slaps the Idiot on the arm. "He goes by the name of the NEWPORT IDIOT," he said. "Picked him up in the New England galaxy. Doesn't know much about sports, but he tries his best."

Suddenly a Bounty Hunter with smooth cappuccino skin dropped into the booth, his blaster pointed at Horn.

The Idiot WAARRRFFF'd.

"Adam Horn," he said. "I have been looking for you."

"I've been looking for you, too, Batista," Horn said casually. "You can tell Alvin the Hutt I have his money.

"You should not have bet against the Lakers ha-ha-haha," the notorious bounty hunter, Christian Batista, chuckled. He lifted the blaster at Horn. "Alvin has promised me a nice bounty for your head, Adam Horn."

Under the table, Horn's finger pressed against the trigger.

The Brown Mosquito nose-dived into Batista's wrist and he fired a laser blast into the wall behind Horn.

Horn BLASTED him.

He said, "You can tell Alvin the only reason the Lakers won that Game 7 was because the suspect referees handed them 20 more free throw attempts in that game, and still only won by 4 points."

"Let's get out of here," the Mosquito said calmly.

"Hey!" the bartender, Goose, shouted. "Hey! Who's gonna pay for this mess?"

Cali Green floated by, pulling his middle-finger out of his shirt pocket and holding it up to Goose. "Keep the change, brah," he laughed on his way out.

The Brown Mosquito bzzzzz'd to the small foyer of the upstairs restaurant. There were merchandise racks with Endless Summer logos on teeshirts, sweatshirts, and hats for sale. An elevator beside the staircase went down to the main entrance level.

"Uh-oh," said Shitbeard. "We've got trouble."

The General Manager of the establishment, Jon, had been alerted of the situation and was headed to the elevator. "This is a big mistake," he muttered. "...messing with me and my time. I am going to take care of this. Yes, I am. You can not shoot someone and leave the body in a booth. No, definitely not. I'm not sure if that's in the handbook. If it's not, then I definitely should add it." He turned and headed for the office. "I should add it in, right now, and give it to the staff at the employee meeting." He stopped and turned back to the elevator. "No, first I should go upstairs and make a formal inspection for my report."

"Quick," TJ watched from the top of the stairs. "Do something!"

Thinking quickly, the Brown Mosquito dove his nose into the elevator "down" button. When the elevator door opened, he grabbed the rack of colorful hats for sale. He dragged it in and buzzed back out. It took up almost the whole elevator car. The elevator light DING'd and the door closed, requested on the first floor.

Jon tapped his foot, waiting. There was only a short flight of stairs, but there was no way he was tackling that Mt. Everest.

They watched from behind the railing bars at the top of the stairs: the Brown Mosquito, Cali Green, Captain Shitbeard, TJ (in a Mesa T's baseball shirt and cap), Adam Horn, and the Newport Idiot.

Downstairs, General Manager Jon paced, waiting for the elevator to arrive.

"I have to call Jordano's back about that last order," he muttered to himself. "I have to do the scheduling, and payroll..."

The door opened and Jon was mortified. "Bop-Bop-Bop-Bop-Bop-Bop!" he somehow stammered out. "A hat rack in the elevator? Who-in-the-how-the-what-who-I mean how — "

"Now's our chance," said the Brown Mosquito. "He can't climb up those stairs. Won't even try anymore. That elevator is his only hope."

"What — how the — how many times — who left the — never leave ah-ah-ah-ah ah hat rack in the elevator!"

Jon struggled to yank the hat rack out.

"Let's go," said Horn. "I know a back staircase."

The six of them ran down the outside stone staircase and into the alley.

The air was calm, with a salty smell from the ocean.

"The ship's up here," said Horn, and he and the Newport Idiot led them across the parking lot.

At a tall chain-linked fence, the moon gave them enough light to find the gate, wrapped in heavy chain. Horn went to the lock and started the combination.

"This ship is not exactly mine. It's my ex-wife's. So just stay low and out of sight, got it?" He dialed the last number and popped open the padlock. He pulled the heavy chain off the fence and pushed open the gate.

"Hurry, come on."

They all entered the boatyard, sailboats high on boat-stands. The moonlight glistened over the sleek white fiberglass hulls above them.

"I said we needed a fast ship," said the Brown Mosquito. "Not a pleasure cruise."

"Keep your pants on, kid. You never heard of the SB CHERRY POPPER?"

"Uh, no," said the Mosquito. "Should I have?"

"She's the fastest ship in the galaxy, broke 6 Cherries before I was 20," Adam Horn flipped his hair in a really cool way. "She's fast enough for you and your little crew of virgins."

"Hey!" shouted the Captain. "You wanna see my dick? Do ya? I'll show ya, right here. Here, look at my balls."

"I put my dick in a tailpipe," said the Newport Idiot.

"Holy shit, it talks!" exclaimed the Captain, stunned by words from the mouth of the animal-like creature.

"Yeah, he doesn't say much," said Horn. "And when he does talk, he usually doesn't make much sense. Think he got hit in the head playing pond hockey in Rhode Island. Alright, here she is."

He stands proudly in front of a spaceship with blinking lights.

"Holy crap, this is yours?" the Brown Mosquito gazed up at it.

"My ex-wife's. Now get aboard before the cameras pick us up."

They run up the ramp into the dim-lit cabin.

Horn and the Newport Idiot make their way past them and up to the cockpit.

"This is far out, man," said Cali Green. "Mind if I do a Jay?"

"Give me some of that shit," roared the Captain. "What else ya got? Mushrooms? Molly? Percocet?"

The Captain took a huge toke of the large joint and handed it back to Cali Green.

"Yeah, man," Cali said. "I got all that shit."

"Good," said the Captain. "I got this." He pulled a bottle of whiskey out of his coat pocket. "And this," he pulled out a bottle of gin in another pocket. "And this," a bottle of vodka in yet another pocket, "And this," a bottle of tequila in another, "And this," a bottle of light rum in one pocket, "And this," a bottle of dark rum in another.

"We'll do an old fashion trade and swap and wash it down with this," he pulled a bottle of Jaegermeister out of another pocket. Where's the ice in this mobile home?"

"In the back," said Adam Horn as he grabbed the controls. The Newport Idiot fired up the engine. "But you're gonna want to hold on." The ship lifted off the ground, rising above the boatyard. "Set coordinates, Idiot. Fantasy Baseball System. ESPN galaxy."

The Newport Idiot looked over the controls, hundreds of blinking lights. "Uhhhhh, which one is it again?" the Idiot asked.

"The button with the dick in the tailpipe," said Horn.

"Oh, that's right," the Idiot said, and pushed the button of a middle-aged man in lingerie sticking his dick in a tailpipe, soon to be his fantasy baseball logo.

The stars rushed at the cockpit window like white lines and the SB Cherry Popper blasted into space.

In the parking lot at the back of the restaurant, two drunk bartenders stumbled out with cans of whipped cream. They pressed their finger lightly on the nozzle and sucked in the fumes.

"Daaaaaaaaaaaaaa," one of them says and uses his whip cream bottle to draw a huge penis on the black cement of the valet parking lot. The other bartender drew huge tits with his whip cream bottle and then dots jizz landing on the huge tits.

WHOOSH — a strong sudden gust of wind as the spaceship takes off.

"What was that?" exclaimed the first bartender.

They watched a blaze of orange streak across the sky.

"Well, that's pretty neat," said the other and laughed and stumbled.

The back door opened and the bartenders scrambled away. It was the General Manager, Jon, on the phone with someone as he thumped down the back stairs.

"Yes, I am aware of that. But my weight is not the issue here," Jon leaned his chin into the phone against his shoulder. "I'll have you know I am on a diet of red meat and bread. It's called the sandwich diet, and it's very successful. I feel like I'm in the best shape of my life. The issue is getting an elevator repairman out here immediately. How am I supposed to run a business if I can't even get upstairs!"

He turned and saw the whipped cream dick and titties depicted in white foamy lines across the valet lot. "Oh, no, oh my, Gene I'm gonna have to call you back. Someone thought it was funny — " he fumbled with the cordless phone as he struggled to turn his body around and grab the handrail with his meaty fingers. "Employees are not permitted to take whipped cream without ringing it in or go into the walk-in without asking permission. They absolutely should not... oh dear." He tried to get that first foot up onto the bottom step but he was having trouble. He took a deep breath and tried again. Nope.

Above in the sky, the stars were countless in the crystal clear night. A light breeze ruffled the flags high on the flag post. A new season dawned.

The Legend of Crazy Fool

Crazy Fool always dressed in black shirts with the sleeves ripped off. His shoulders and arms were buff from paddling through heavy surf on his bodyboard, which he always held at his side. He had the look of someone who could kick your ass, but that anxiety went away when you heard him laugh. He wore spiked bracelets, kept his hair short and tight with a short, horned spike and a trim goatee.

If you'd ask him, he'd tell you his favorite team was the Raiders. Silver and Black all the way. But he did have a soft spot for the San Diego Padres, that sad local team that always gave the fans of southern California hope. Around the All-Star Break, that hope would crash like a wave at Swami's, leaving the city with an endless second half of meaningless baseball.

Crazy Fool was realistic. That ball club would never win. Not with the strategy they employed. The Padres had given up trying to keep up with the big city markets, so he assumed the team had just given up altogether. Crazy Fool knew a brand new approach must be made. They had to think outside the box. A revolutionary analysis called Sabermetrics was being discussed in clubhouses around the league. There was new thought to how baseball players could be analyzed and valued. But the Padres were stuck in the dark ages, and made terrible decisions, like letting Anthony Rizzo get away.

Crazy Fool had body-surfed every beach in southern California. But he knew there was more out there. He knew he could create a better baseball world. If only given the chance. But why bother, he thought. Raider season was coming up. And that's all that really mattered.

One day, he was at a barbecue at his cousin's house in Carlsbad. There was a huge spread of food on the long tables outside and light conversation among friends and family. The ocean breeze ruffled above in the tall palm trees. Some musicians were setting up at the other end of the yard.

"What up, brotha'?"

"What up Tre," Crazy Fool slapped his cousin the California bro-hug.

"Place is dope, man," said Crazy Fool.

"Yeah. Just got me some new woofers," said his cousin.

Huge speakers were being lifted high on stands as the band's crew worked on the outdoor stage.

"Yeah, I see that," said Fool.

"Nah, these woofers, man." Two identical bulldogs ambled through the party crowd.

"Ah," laughed Crazy Fool. "Nice, man."

"Ah, Hell, nah," his cousin suddenly exclaimed when he noticed someone walking through the party.

A tall skinny "woman" limped gingerly across the grass in high heels.

"Who the Hell is that?" asked Crazy Fool.

"That is one mean bitch," his cousin chewed on a toothpick. "Goes by San Francisco Tranny On Crak. You do not wanna mess with him."

"That's a him? You sure?"

SF Tranny on Crak turned and peeled towards them, going any which direction her heels twisted in the grass.

"Nah, she's a dude, for 'sho," said his cousin, "but don't let her hear you say it. She will whup yo ass."

SF Tranny on Crak was practically on top of them when she pea-cocked, "Hiiiiiiiii, I'm Tranny."

She stuck out her long spindly fingers with long fake nails. She had a fluffy collar on a jacket that stopped just short of her belly and dangling jewelry that jingled as she reached her hand towards him.

Crazy Fool lifted his hand, unsure. SF Tranny grabbed it hard and shook it.

"Hiiiiiii, Bonny," she tried to plant a kiss on Crazy Fool's cousin but he shoved her away.

"Get away from me you crazy bitch! And don't call me that!"

"I am a crazy bitch! And someone told me this fine handsome gentleman is Crazy Fool. What'd ya know?"

"Yo, I ain't crazy like that, you know what I'm sayin'?" Crazy Fool backed off.

"Don't be scared, sugar. I can take you places you ain't never been before." Her giant red lips pursed as she undressed him with her eyes.

With a screeching JOLT the music started; a quick and clean electric guitar riff, and then it dropped into a slow, thumping pulse, warranting cheers and shouts from the party as heads begin to bob.

"Damn, dude," Crazy Fool bounced as the rhythm kicked in, and then the lyrical flow of the singer. "This shit is tight."

"Yeah, they're from Long Beach," said his cousin. "They're called Sublime."

After the show, Crazy Fool stumbled around the party holding onto a 40 ounce. The yard was littered with paper plates and red plastic cups that were smashed underfoot. Crazy Fool landed at the keg, a blunt hanging from his lips. "Anything left in there?" he slurred and began pumping the tap. He put the spout into the neck of the 40 bottle and filled it up.

He saw the band loading their equipment into their van. Crazy Fool walked over and leaned against a tree, puffing his joint.

"That the last one?" a band member asked as an amp was loaded in.

From inside the driver said, "Awe, man. It smells like Lou Dog inside the van."

"Alright, let go," said Bradley, the lead singer. "Here we come, Ventura."

A bolt of lightning struck Crazy Fool in the heart and he'll never know why he did what he did next. It was probably the booze, and the smoke, but something prompted him to suddenly shout:

"Yo! You going to Ventura?"

"Yeah, man," said Bradley. "Gotta show up there tomorrow night."

"Yo, you think you can drop me in Oxnard?"

"Why you wanna go there?"

"Hustlin.' Trying to make that cash, homie. I won't any be trouble, man. Just me and my board."

"Yeah, it's cool, man. You get next to Lou Dog."

"I'm coming, tooooooo!" The SF Tranny on Crack ran to the van in long high-heeled jaunts.

"No, no way!" Crazy Fool tried to stop her.

"You keep those dirty hands off me, mister or I will yell rape!"

"You are a crazy bitch."

"And you are a crazy fool! Bradley! Brad-ley. I have your honey pot."

"Oh, yeah, you know it, sweet mama," Bradley cooed in a raspy voice from singing all night. "What you got for me, Tranny?"

She carefully walks over to him and opens her purse.

"Got all a' that candy sweeter than sugar," she said, her purse full of narcotics.

"Alright, make room for one more," Bradley announced to the band.

So, Sublime, Crazy Fool, and SF Tranny on Crack all loaded in and they took off for the 101. The back of the van was actually quite comfortable. There were small couches and pillows and a dog bed and lots of guitars.

SF Tranny handed the bandmates the heroin, and they cooked it up right there.

She sat down next to Crazy Fool. "For you, darling, I think something a little more, fun."

"I'm good," said Crazy Fool. "I don't shoot that shit."

"No, no, no, of course not. Something mellow. Just a taste."

She reached into her bag and pulled out... an unopened pack of baseball cards.

"Baseball cards?" Crazy Fool looked at her like she was crazy, and she was. Probably crazier than him.

"Open them," she said.

Crazy Fool shook his head, but he opened them. Flipped through the players. He even knew some of 'em. And then, after the last one, something thin fell into his hand.

A stiff stick of bubblegum.

He looked up at her. "Chew it," she said.

"How long has it been in there?" he asked.

"A long, long time," she said and rested against the van as it thumped through the streets. It'll let you see things you never thought possible. Here, let's split it."

Crazy Fool snapped the stick of gum and handed her half.

"You ready to take on the Big Leagues?" she asked him.

The van accelerated onto the onramp as Crazy Fool stuck the gum into his mouth. It sped up faster and faster onto the highway. He stared at the ceiling, a blast of energy trickling through his bones. SF Tranny grabbed his hand and they rocketed off into the cosmos, the stars became white lines as they blasted away.

Finding Big Mac

The SB Cherry Popper raced through the universe, a trail of fire from her thrusters blazed across the ink and stars of the perpetual night of outer-space.

"Ok, hold on everyone. We're going in," Adam Horn guided the controls towards a blue planet, lowering his altitude into thick atmospheric clouds.

The Newport Idiot adjusted the ship's speed.

"WAAAAARRRRFFF!"

"Alright, Idiot, power down the rear thrusters and increase wing throttle," said Horn.

The large creature handled the controls with experience. Horn picked up the transmitter.

"Echo One, Echo One, this is the SB CHERRY POPPER. We are approaching from the North-Northwest."

"Roger that, SB Cherry Popper. You have permission to continue," the radio cackled.

Horn shut off the transmitter, flipped on the in-ship intercom as the hull started to shake with the turbulence of a system of clouds.

"Alright we're coming in," Horn said on the intercom. "You may want to get strapped down back there."

Nothing but radio static.

He looked at the Idiot, and then again, "Hello? Anybody still back there?"

Quiet but for the static. The Idiot shrugged.

In the back of the ship, Def Leppard's "Pour Some Sugar On Me" was blaring.

Colorful lights flashed in the Hawaiian Shirt pattern of the ceiling. Girls danced on the bar.

Captain Shitbeard poured himself another Jaeger shot and SHOUTED an indecipherable exclamation.

The Brown Mosquito was lining up races at the end of the bar, two straws in each cocktail.

Below a glowing sign "CHOWDER LOUNGE," four beautiful girls took the drinks. They cheer the Brown Mosquito, and then take them down to pound-town.

TJ was passed out drunk, drool reaching close to his shoulder.

Cali Green danced by himself with round green sunglasses on. "Pour Some Sugar on MEEEE!!" he sings and plays air guitar.

The whole ship rattled as the turbulence grew more intense. The lights and music flickered, the floor shook, glasses jingled.

"I'll do one," the Captain held up a finger when he heard the jingling of the glasses and he poured himself another shot.

In the cockpit, Adam Horn held tight to the controls.

"WAAAARRR!" the Idiot said but it was too late.

The clouds thinned and dissipated and straight ahead appeared…

THE GIANT CURVED WALL OF THE ST. LOUIS ARCH!

Horn pushed forward as hard as he could, diving the ship vertically under the enormous stone monument, gritting his teeth as he tried to clear underneath it.

Suddenly, the back room lost gravity – and everyone and everything started floating.

"Far out, maaan," Cali Green grinned as he slowly flipped backward. "Far fucking out."

The liquid Jaegermeister floated out of Captain Shitbeard's shot glass in a congealed form.

"Ho, ho, ho, ho, ho," the Captain said, and swam towards the floating liquor with his bearded lips pursed like a fish.

In the cockpit, Adam Horn just cleared the bottom of the St. Louis Arch and pulled back up as the ground quickly approached.

"We're coming in too fast, Idiot. Release all thrusters."

The SB Cherry Popper screamed through the sky toward a major metropolis.

Horn tried to gain altitude as they raced over a city of hundreds of thousands of people.

"WAAAARRRRRRFFF!" the Idiot shouted.

"I'm trying, Idiot!" he shouted back.

The spacecraft rocketed over the freeway, barely clearing cars.

Horn spun the ship to dodge a skyscraper and flew down a street just over the roofs of taxis and buses.

A mother walking a baby looked up as the ship CRACKED OPEN the sky.

Horn held on as the ship BUMP, BUMP, BOUNCED over the highway, slowing down but not fast enough. A large brick building was up ahead and closing fast.

"HOLD ON!" shouted Horn.

The ship SLAMMED into the building and brick crumbled down upon it.

In the back room, the passengers were JOLTED upon impact.

Horn and the Idiot were thrown over the controls, dust and sparks raining down on them.

Finally at rest, Adam Horn coughed in the thick dust, looked up through the windshield as bricks continued to trickle down over it.

"Wow. That was close," he said. Then he looked at the Idiot. "How's my hair?"

The crew all wobbled out of the smoking ship into the bright daylight. The towering crumbling brick wall above them read, "Busch Stadium."

"We're here! We made it," TJ was in awe. "This is where the St. Louis Cardinals play! Adam Wainwright, Albert Pujols, Yaddy Molina... They won the World Series in 2006 in five games over the Tigers."

"Well, then, let's go plunder some of their players," said Captain Shitbeard.

The Brown Mosquito was awakened by an indeterminate feeling. "I know this place," he said. "I've been here before." He couldn't quite pinpoint the feeling, and it lingered.

"If you want to start a league, we'll have to go to the fantasy baseball offices of ESPN," Horn explained. "They'll have the answers you're looking for."

They walked up the street away from the stadium. The Brown Mosquito looked back, knowing someday that he would return.

"You better let me do the talking," said Horn. "These are some pretty unsavory characters. Led by a man you do not want to mess around with."

"Worse than Alvin the Hutt?" asked the Brown Mosquito.

"Some call him Satan," said Horn. "Kid, this might be the most evil person in the entire universe. I've never met anyone else so downright cold in their bones."

The Captain piped up, “Who is this unspeakable land creature?”

“They call him Big Mac,” Horn said and nodded to a billboard above them.

Bright red block letters on the billboard shouted:

St. Louis,
Home of Major League Baseball’s Home Run King

Mark McGwire!

A Record 70 Home Runs in One Season!

Big Mac’s fat red face almost popped out from the billboard, with what looked like a wad of tobacco in his cheek.

Someone had graffitied on it “CHEATER!”

Police sirens announced themselves several blocks away.

“Let’s get outta here,” said Horn.

As they hurried across the street, the Brown Mosquito could not escape this déjà vu feeling. That this all seemed very familiar. He looked back up at Big Mac. He reminded the Mosquito of someone. But who?

Captain Shitbeard suddenly started sprinting full speed. A city bus was pulling up to a stop. The Captain unsheathed his sword as he ran towards it.

"ARRRRRGH!!" he yelled as he jumped into the bus.

Everyone screamed when they saw his sword.

"Everyone off! This ship is being commandeered by the notorious Captain SHITBEARD! Unless you choose to sail with me in me crew, then this will be yar' final opportunity ta walk tha plank!"

One-by-one the passengers exited, the Captain making them "jump" off the plank onto the sidewalk at sword-point.

The Brown Mosquito, TJ, Cali Green, Adam Horn, and the Newport Idiot all piled in.

The Captain got behind the wheel. "Got a light West breeze behind us, looks like flat seas ahead. Untie us, Idiot, so we can ride the next swell going out!"

The Idiot WAARRRRFFFFFF'd.

The bus JOLTED into the street, zigged and zagged and clipped a parked car and nearly hit another coming the other way.

"ARRRRGGGHH!!!!" the Captain waved a middle finger out the window at the car HONKING past him.

The bus rumbled ahead, dodging traffic. Above the brick factory was the billboard, and Big Mac's giant red pock-marked face.

The Theatre of Fantasy Baseball

Darkness engulfed him even after Crazy Fool blinked his eyes open.

"Hello? Hello?" His voice echoed in the chamber.

His head was killing him. Pounding. What was that smell? He couldn't understand how it could be so dark. Was he blind?

"The stick of gum!" he thought out loud. "That crazy bitch! She blinded me!"

He felt around in the dark. Something slimy recoiled his hand. Some kind of box fell against his foot. What the fuck was that smell? Crazy Fool tried to stand but there was no solid footing. He tried to get ahold of something, but he touched that slime again! He jerked his head and it SLAMMED against something hard.

"Fuck!" Crazy Fool rubbed his head. And then his hand searched for what he hit. Something metal. He pushed it up, bringing light into his world.

Crazy Fool lifted the lid of the dumpster, looked out into the alley. Cars honked out in the street. The other end of the alley was blocked off by a gate.

A dumpster lid across from him started to lift, and SF Tranny on Crak poked his/her head out. "Mornin'," she said.

Crazy Fool shook garbage off of himself and climbed out.

"What the fuck are we doing in dumpsters?" he asked, annoyed at even having to acknowledge her.

"Sleeping, silly," SF Tranny stretched. "Even big tough guys like you need your beauty sleep."

"But why in a dumpster?"

"Why not?" she answered. "That's where I always sleep. It's quiet and soft, and no one bothers you. The best part is it's rent-free! I didn't pay a dime to sleep here last night!"

SF Tranny on Crak used her buff arms and shoulders to pull herself up and out of the dumpster and she swung her long shaved leg over the edge.

"You want to get some breakfast, or did you already eat?" she asked.

"Already eat? In there?" he looked back at the dumpster.

"I found a bagel," she said proudly. "And some sauce. Not sure what it was. White and salty."

"You are disgusting," said Crazy Fool.

"Oh please, honey. I forgot you were spoon-fed caviar as a baby. Well, ok, then, we could go to the Four Seasons for a champagne brunch and crab legs. I don't know. How is what I'm wearing?"

"I didn't grow up rich. I've worked for everything I got! Now where the Hell are we?"

"The big CITY!" Tranny said with flair.

He walked to the corner to check out the busy street. Tranny wobbled in her high heels behind him.

"L.A.?" he asked.

"No," she said. "We blew right through L.A. and straight out of California, we circled the globe a few times, and then landed here."

"What the fuck?"

"Listen, you wanted to make it big, right? Make some real money? Well, here we are. In the center of all the action! The entertainment! The shopping! The night-life! The big time!"

“Big time? More like Slum Dog.” The street reeked of garbage. And so did they. People gave them a wide berth as they walked past pawn shops, boarded up apartments, and thrift stores.

“To find our way in the big city we need to find our niché, Crazy Fool,” she fluffed her boa back around her neck. It whooshed across Fool's face and he swatted it away. She was about a head taller than him and her long strides made him hurry to keep up.

“To make it big you need to find something that makes you special, unique, extra-ordinary! Tell me Crazy Fool, what is it that makes you special? Do you have any secret talents?”

He held up his sponge body-board, attached by the leash to his wrist.

“A boogie-board?” she exclaimed. “Ohhhh. How exciting!”

“It’s not a boogie-board!” Crazy Fool shouted. “It’s a body-board! And yeah I fucking shred. Where the hell am I gonna do that here? All I see is concrete!”

“Come' on, darling, I know just the place. Where the lights are brightest. A theatre of drama and tragedy. Where the actors are known around the world.”

“Fuck no I’m not going to the theatre,” Crazy Fool stopped. “I’d rather go back in the dumpster.”

"Darling, the theatre is where all the magic happens! The colorful outfits! The choreography! The graceful dance of men coming together as one!"

"You have fun with your dancing men," Crazy Fool turned and walked the other way. "I'm outta here. No way am I getting on stage for some stupid play."

"It's not a stupid play, Crazy Fool," she said, and walking away said almost out of ear-shot, "And the stage is a diamond. A beautiful baseball diamond."

"Baseball?" that stopped him in his tracks.

Before she turned the corner she shouted, "It's Fantasy, darling."

Crazy Fool thought it over. "Fantasy? Baseball?"

He suddenly was jolted into action. "Wait!" he shouted after her. "Tranny! Wait!"

He ran to the corner, knocking people aside with his body-board.

He finally caught up to her on the next block, breathing heavily. "I'm in!" he shouted.

"You're not ready," she scoffed and continued her long strides.

"I am ready!" he said. "I'll do whatever it takes!"

She stopped and looked him up and down. "Those savages in fantasy baseball will eat you alive. I need to get you into shape. And it starts with the mind. Here, smoke this."

She handed him a one-hitter meant to look like a cigarette.

"What? Here?" People passed them.

"I knew you weren't ready," she said.

"Yo, who you talkin' to? I'm Crazy Fool! I don't give a fuuck." he took it and puffed the one-hitter, coughed a little. Swirls of colors like giant lolly-pops twirled around. Crazy Fool's feet lifted off the ground.

"What is this?" he said, blurry-eyed.

Up ahead, SF Tranny on Crak floated above him. She rose toward the pink clouds and Crazy Fool swam through the sky after her.

"We're going to Fantasy Land!" she shouted and soared into the clouds.

Partnership Formed

A lone rooster clucked and pecked through an empty early morning street. A door slammed open against a wall, the front door of a neighborhood bar called The Cliff Room. Cali Green stumbled out. Adam Horn slammed into the open door after him, drunk as shit.

The Brown Mosquito and Captain Shitbeard were right behind, zig-zag steps leading them right out of the bar.

The door closed but the Newport Idiot kicked it back open, carrying TJ in his arms.

"DAAAAAAARRRR!" the Idiot shouted out into the early morning fog.

"Bear Fight, Bear Fight," Horn muttered in some kind of trauma as he recounted the last five shots he did.

"Bonsai... Motor... Speedway," mumbled the Brown Mosquito and he loudly burped a green cloud.

“Nnnnnnnoraaaaaa, the Exploraaaaaaa,” Cali Green stumbled and almost lost his balance into the bushes, but Captain Shitbeard is right there behind him to shove him all the way in.

“Ha!” the Mosquito laughed as Cali Green tried to get out of the shrubs like a beetle on it’s back..

The Mosquito turned his sights to the Newport Idiot. Though he was much, much smaller, he body-slammed the Idiot with extreme drunk force. The Idiot didn't have a chance and went flying into the bushes. TJ flung out of his arms.

“Daaaaaaaa,” the Mosquito buzzed around in looping Cosby impressions.

Cali Green picked little sticks out of his hair. “Which way do we go, man?” he asked.

“I know, I know,” said Horn. “This way I think.” He stumbled forward down the street.

TJ peeled a dirty sock off his ball cap from the garbage can he landed in, and gets up after them as fast as his little legs could go.

The early morning rush hour was just beginning as the team of hammerheads made their way into the business district of the city. Skyscrapers towered over them.

They walked up to a glass building at the top of a long set of stairs.

"This is it," said Adam Horn. "This is where the magic happens."

"Magic, ha," mumbled a homeless man, and covers his nose with a blanket. "The only magic in there is greed!"

The Mosquito looked from him up the long flight of stairs to the blinding sunlight reflected off huge glass windows.

Through his round, green-tinted glasses, Cali Green looked up in awe.

TJ's eyes widened as he gazed up at the big sign:

ESPN HEADQUARTERS

A couple of men in suits on their way in to work jogged up the stairs to the entrance.

"Well," said Captain Shitbeard as he put a dip in his mouth. "I hope we're not over-dressed."

The Captain reached down and picked up the rusty tin can on the ground next to the homeless man. He jingled the two or three coins in the can and then SPLAT dip-juice into it.

Only the sleeping homeless man's thinning tuft of hair stuck out from under his blanket, as the bejeweled fingers of the Captain placed a $20 bill next to him.

They were about to walk up the stairs into the ESPN offices when Crazy Fool and SF Tranny on Crak approached from the other direction.

They all stared at each other, sizing each other up.

"You going in there?" asked Crazy Fool.

"Hell, yeah we're going in," replied the Captain. "Didn't realize it was a freak show audition."

SF Tranny stepped in front of Crazy Fool before he went full-on crazy on the Captain.

"Now just wait a minute, mister scruffle-puff," Tranny bellowed. "The two of us have more fantasy baseball talent in this long pinky fingernail of mine that I sometimes use as a spoon than you do in your entire gorgeous, vintage pirate costume. Are those real feathers? This cuff-work is fantastic."

The Brown Mosquito knew they needed more managers. Ten to be exact. And he had a feeling about these two. "You go in with us, we play by our rules," the Brown Mosquito said.

"Well, now, aren't you a darling? And such a long stinger," SF Tranny gushed.

"No gay stuff!" the Mosquito roared back. "Ten owners. A hundred each. Five hundred bucks for the winner of the Championship, runner-up gets two-hundred."

"What about the other three hundred?" asked Crazy Fool.

"It goes to the winner of the Pennant," said TJ, making himself seen through the legs of the bigger men. "The best regular-season record wins the Pennant and three-hundred dollars."

"What about advanced stats?" asked Crazy Fool. "I'm not wasting my time with standard accounting."

Adam Horn said, "For the pitchers, there's extra points for shutouts, complete games, no-hitters, and you get get one point for each inning pitched. We're bumping it up to two points for a strikeout, but negative two for giving up an earned run."

Crazy Fool nodded to SF Tranny.

Very unexpectedly, the Newport Idiot perfectly articulated, "Batters get the standard one point for a hit, two for doubles, and so on, but we've added bonus points for Grand-Slams, hitting for the cycle, turning a Double Play, Game-Winning RBI, and two points for when a player's major league team wins, taking into account the intangibles your player brings to his team."

They all stand dumbfounded, staring at the suddenly well-spoken Newport Idiot. He shrugged his shoulders and groaned, "WAAAARRFFFF?"

"Sounds like they'll be some high scoring matchups," said SF Tranny.

"One more thing," said the Brown Mosquito. "Your team fee is due the day of the draft. One month from the draft date it will go up ten dollars and continue to go up ten dollars every month it is not paid. The accumulation of these fees will go to the winner of the Championship."

SF Tranny grabbed Crazy Fool by the shoulders. "This is it, Crazy Fool! This is your dream! To use your special talents and become the fantasy baseball owner you always knew you could be!"

Crazy Fool put his body-board down and stuck his hand out, shaking hands with the Brown Mosquito.

They all began the long walk up the stairs to the entrance.

Crazy Fool and the Newport Idiot pulled open the large glass doors and one-by-one they all walked into the offices of ESPN Headquarters.

ESPN FANTASY BASEBALL OFFICES

The sight was overwhelming. Data was everywhere. Lines and lines of computerized digits in green, white, black or red. Brown Mosquito was amazed at all the number crunching going on, on screens large and small and on smartphones pulled from pockets. Men and women sat at desks, looking up stats, compiling lists, typing notes and columns and draft strategies and injury reports and minor league prospect reports.

"Wow," said the Brown Mosquito. "Fantasy Baseball has come a long way. Look at all these numbers.

"Aye," said the Captain. "They've built a fortress out of them."

"I think I'm going to draft a catcher first," said the Newport Idiot. "That's always a good idea. Then a relief pitcher."

Adam Horn peered over the shoulder of someone at a desk and read his computer screen:

2009 Fantasy Preview Top 100

1. Hanley Ramirez
2. Albert Pujols
3. David Wright
4. Jose Reyes
5. Ryan Braun
6. Miguel Cabrera

Horn is bumped from behind by Captain Shitbeard and keeps moving.

The Brown Mosquito grabbed glimpses of data and reports:

- Josh Hamilton: could be in store for mammoth '09 numbers...
- Ryan Howard: bank on massive HR numbers, RBI totals...
- Alfonso Soriano: five category stud. One of the game's best when healthy...

Hundreds of names. Billions of numbers.

An enormous screen on the far wall digitally updated the fantasy universe. All the leagues from around the world were drafting their teams.

The Brown Mosquito looked up at the hundreds and hundreds of leagues.

"There's only one number at the top, is what I say," the Captain bumped into him from behind and spoke softly. "I say we take it all. Winner gets the entire plunder. No reward for second place. What d'ya say?"

"THAT'S WHAT I SAY. NO REWARD FOR SECOND PLACE," the parrot on his shoulder repeats.

"Keep it DOWN, Little Mikey, Jr.!" the Captain barked at his parrot. "We don't know if there could be ears around here."

They walked past researchers with headphones on, typing on computers and occasionally pushing up their glasses.

"Ah, here we are," said Horn as they came to an open reception room labeled "Start a New League."

A receptionist stopped them from going through the doors. "Please sign in with your ESPN account."

"Huh?" the Captain sneered. "We don't use computers! How dumb do you think we are?!"

“Let me handle this, Captain Shitbeard,” said the boy, TJ, as he put a reassuring hand on his arm. “I’ve used a computer before.”

“Go to the visitor computer station and fill out the forms.”

TJ sat at a desk and wiggled his way in. He turned on the laptop in front of him and stared at the screen. Then he started typing. User name, password, security question in case he forgot his password, the last four digits of his social, and his favorite sports teams, one-by-one, in each sport.

“Let’s get on with it!” shouted the Captain. “One more minute in the belly of this concrete beast and I’ll start taking hostages! Why is there no bar in here?”

“Almost there,” said TJ as he furiously typed. “What’s the name of our league?”

Everyone looked at the Brown Mosquito.

“Satan’s Bullpen,” he said, not really sure how or why but he liked the sound of it.

“Ok,” said TJ and typed. Under “Team Name” he pecked the keyboard to spell: MESA T’S.

The Brown Mosquito was on another laptop and typed: BROWN MOSQUITOS. Then he ripped a slow, long, nasty buzzing fart, producing a cloud of putrid air as it bzzzzzzzzzzzzzzz’d all across the room.

“Argggghh!” they complain and cough.

Cali Green coughed and spit. "Nothing worse than a Brown Mosquito in your mouth."

"Ah! Get me outta here!" the Captain roared, pulling out a bottle of Jaeger. "Where is the air in this devil box?"

"Yeah, man, why don't you guys plant some trees in here or something?" Cali Green covered his nose with his old baseball jersey with "Cali Green" scripted across the chest.

"Baseball is about being outdoors! In the fresh air!" the Captain Shouted, getting angrier. His lazy eye started wandering.

"No," said Crazy Fool. "This is the way. We have to play by their rules. With their computer system. Did you see all the competitors on that big screen in there? This is it! This is where we make our mark!"

"Aye," said the Captain. "And we shall claim glory and fame. But what I have learned in my own experience is the only way to find glory and fame is to play by your own rules!"

He pulls out a cork from a whiskey bottle with his teeth and spits it out.

"No one is making Captain Shitbeard use a computer." He chugged the whiskey; one gulp, two, three, four, five. He breathed heavily and wiped his bearded mouth on his sleeve.

"No, sir! Wait!" the secretary failed to stop him as Shitbeard KICKED through the doors.

"ARRRRRRGGGH!!!"

He has interrupted a meeting, and the well-dressed executives didn't look too happy about it.

The Mosquito buzzed in right after and immediately thought it was strange how large the men were. Almost giants.

Thick necks. Muscles bulging through the fabric of their suits. Large heads. The biggest one of them all sat at the head of the table. He was almost a giant, even when sitting down.

There was a nameplate before him: Rafael Palmeiro.

"What is the meaning of this?" Palmeiro boomed as Captain Shitbeard marched up to the titan with his sword drawn.

"You the captain of this boardroom?" Shitbeard demanded. "We be taking the helm of this fantasy league, and be playing by our own rules. And if you try to stop us, ya'll be findin' yar'self at the bottom of Andruw Jones locker."

Palmeiro pushed a button under the desk. "What exactly do you want?" he asked, very calmly, his giant mustache barely moving. His hair was perfect, but in a hat-hair kind of way.

The Captain looked back at the crew. "What exactly do we want?" he shouted back at them.

"There are a few changes we'd like to make," TJ ambled forward. "To the rules and rosters specifically."

"Yeah, man," said Cali Green, "like 2 points for a strikeout."

The executives all looked at each other with confused looks and chuckles.

Palmeiro's huge mustache shifted as he said, "Fine."

Shitbeard took a piss in a plant in the corner. "And we want to start 5 outfielders!"

"Fine," said Palmeiro. "Is that all?"

"Mr. Palmeiro?" TJ stepped forward. "Mr. Rafael Palmeiro?"

The man's melon-sized eyes rolled down to the boy.

"Raffy Palmeiro, who hit .324 in 1999? With 47 Home Runs? And 148 RBI?"

Palmeiro smiled upon hearing his prized stats. "Yes," he said and smiled.

"Wow, your numbers really spiked in the late '90s and early 2000's," TJ continued. "Is it true, Mr. Palmeiro, that you took steroids to bulk up those stats?"

Palmeiro's smile disappeared, he glared back down at the boy, his face getting redder and redder.

The threads on the sleeve of his jacket started to pop as his giant biceps bulged.

"You totally cheated," said SF Tranny.

"Yeah, you totally did, man," said Cali. "You cheated."

"You ruined this game!"

"Disgrace."

"Cheater!"

"Say it ain't so, Raffy," TJ had tears in his eyes.

A large team of ESPN security rushed in and surrounded them.

Palmeiro glared at the Brown Mosquito. "Access... Denied."

A security guard grabbed Cali Green.

"ARRRRGGGGHH!!" The Captain whipped around and fought back three security guards with his sword. The others were seized with their arms held tight behind their backs.

A security guard grabbed a pool cue and SPLINTERED it across Shitbeard's face (just like that time at the Cliff Room) and the Captain went down.

He was pounced on by the guards, and all of them were dragged out of the office.

Out in the sunlight of a beautiful St. Louis afternoon, the fantasy crew-members were thrown down the stairs all the way down to the sidewalk.

Crazy Fool was just agile enough to get his body-board under him and he rode the rail all the way down to the street.

The Brown Mosquito crashed hard down the stone steps, bruising his wings and his needle-nose badly. He finally came to stop at the wool blanket, with some books and other things that belonged to the homeless man from before.

The Mosquito looked up and saw the same man now sitting across the street at a park bench, reading a newspaper.

The man pulled the paper down and looked over it at him. There was a twinkle in his eye.

Adam Horn rubbed the large bump on his head. Cali Green was lying awkwardly on his back. Captain Shitbeard passed around a bottle of Crown Royale. He pulled out a breaded chicken finger out of his thick beard and took a bite.

They nursed their injuries, dejected, wondering why, and how, and realizing that this dream may be over.

Curious, the Brown Mosquito limped over toward the man on the park bench — limped because his wing was so badly damaged he didn't think he could fly. The man's face was hidden behind the open sports section.

“Fantasy, right?” said the man from behind the newspaper.

“Doesn’t look like it at this point,” the Mosquito sat down next to him. “We’ll never be allowed back in there.”

“Naw, wouldn’t think so,” the man flipped the page but the Mosquito only caught a glimpse of his face.

The Brown Mosquito slumped into his fist. “This is all I ever wanted. I don’t know where to turn now,” he said. “There’s just gotta be a way.”

“Gotta be a way,” repeated the man. “Looks like Louisville has themselves another good squad this year,” he said as he browsed an article. “Gearing up for the big Tournament.”

The Mosquito gazed up at the large glass-paneled front entrance and the big ESPN sign on the shoe-box shaped building across the street.

“All I ever wanted was to feel the magic of owning a real team,” said the Mosquito.

“Well, then, you’re going about it the wrong way,” said the man. “I told you there’s no magic in that building. Let me ask you this. What is the most important factor in putting together a good fantasy baseball team?”

“The stats,” said the Brown Mosquito. “Numbers.”

“That’s true,” said the man. “And that building over there sure has a lot of those, but the numbers don’t make the team. The players do.”

The man eased down the paper, revealing a soft, friendly face.

“Ozzie Smith?” the Mosquito’s eyes bugged out.

When the old ballplayer smiled, instantly he knew it couldn’t be any other.

“You want to see magic?” asked Ozzie. He folded up the paper. “I can show you the magic.”

The twinkle in his eye made the Brown Mosquito believe him.

The Wizard of Oz

The Brown Mosquito followed Ozzie Smith as he led him through the city. The others were too pissed off and beat up and hungover to follow some homeless man through the streets of St. Louis, so they let the Brown Mosquito go off alone.

Ozzie kept a quick pace, and the injured Mosquito hobbled after, trying to keep up.

"I used to get all my stats from the newspaper," Ozzie was saying. "I added up the fantasy calculations on paper, then typed it all up on my old Smith-Corona." Ozzie walked quickly. "Head-to-head matchups, updates, standings. Folded 'em up, put 'em in nine different envelopes each with a stamp and dropped 'em in the blue mailbox at the corner."

The Brown Mosquito almost got trampled by a family with a stroller. He buzzed up and down on the sidewalk but couldn't sustain flight. "You did all that?" he asked.

"Every Monday," said Ozzie. "Went through every line of every box score. Adding the home runs, hits, RBI, strikeouts. Soon I started to see the game in a whole new way. Like the players were right there, right in front of me."

"Ozzie," the Brown Mosquito pleaded. "You played in the major leagues for 18 years. You were an All-Star for 15 of 'em. Of course, the players were right in front of you!"

The Mosquito dodged and ran in zig-zag lines, trying not to get trampled by the large legs swinging all around him.

"No, man. The players I drafted. Playing for me. They came alive. Right there in the boxscore. I could see them. Soon you will, too."

They crossed the street and walked half a block to a shop with white paneled windows. Ozzie opened the door.

Rows and rows and rows of baseball cards in boxes were lined to the far back wall of a huge baseball card shop. The Brown Mosquito followed Ozzie in.

Ozzie flipped through a few cards, then went to another stack, flipped through those. The Mosquito watched him as he expertly flipped the thin cardboard cards like his fingers were playing Spanish guitar. He was looking for something specific. Then he plucked one out.

"David Wright," said Ozzie. "Third-base. Nice."

He took the card with him and went to another stack.

He flipped through another row. Looking, looking, then boom, "Jimmy Rollins," he said. "Shortstop. There we go. Got a soft spot for the shortstops, you know," he said.

The Brown Mosquito went to his own row, flipped through the endless baseball cards. Elvis Andrus, Homer Bailey, Milton Bradley, Troy Glaus, J.J. Hardy, Heath Bell.

The Mosquito sighed as nothing looked appealing. He checked out another row. Flip, flip, flip. Suddenly he stopped. A bit of magic sprinkled over him. Frozen, he carefully pulled a single card out from the thousands of others. Pictured on it, the player was cocked and loaded to drive a fastball deep. He had on a white uniform, and a navy blue helmet with pine tar smudged across the classic "D" emblem of Detroit, and the fierce look of a man who assaults baseballs.

The strip at the bottom read: 1B MIGUEL CABRERA, TIGERS.

The magic sprinkled so thick it was difficult to see anything else, and the Brown Mosquito knew he had just made his first selection.

He looked up for Ozzie, but he was gone.

He went to another row, flipping furiously now. No, no, no, no, no. He picked one up and read the stats on the back. "Nah," he put it back.

More flipping until a skinny young pitcher caught his eye.

Tim Lincecum. San Francisco Giants. Now he had something. He immediately started searching for his next pick and, glancing up, became aware that he was not alone.

He slowly turned around and realized there was someone right behind him. A ballplayer.

"Hey, skip," he said.

"You're…" the Brown Mosquito couldn't believe his eyes.

"I'm Tim Lincecum, but everyone calls me Timmy," said the ballplayer, short and lean with long hair tucked under a ball cap. "You're doing great so far," he said. Taking a power hitter like Miggy in the first round was a solid choice."

Behind Lincecum, Miguel Cabrera waved. They were wearing the same uniform; the brown and yellow of the Brown Mosquitos, and they each wore brown hats with the Mosquito logo.

"Better get back to it," said Timmy. "Your pick is almost up."

Just then the Brown Mosquito noticed that there were others in the baseball card shop.

Captain Shitbeard made eye contact as he lurked in the back, flipping through rows of cards. Cali Green was there, too.

And was that...? A ball cap was all you could see behind the rows of baseball cards, but TJ would reach up and grab a pile, bring them down to his level, and then flip through the cards in his hands.

The Brown Mosquito flipped through more furiously, quickly assembling his team. He turned cards over, looking at the stats on the back.

"Good power, but strikes out a lot," he thought, trying to decide. Crazy Fool was also there. And SF Tranny on Crak. The Newport Idiot. Adam Horn.

Then there were two others that the Brown Mosquito didn't recognize at first, Happy HairyBalls and Team Rosebudd. They, too, were looking through the stacks and collecting their own teams.

The Mosquito hurried. He took an outfielder, and then another pitcher, and passed on a catcher.

"I'll get one later," the Mosquito assured himself.

When he was finished he had a whole team assembled. Five starting pitchers, five starting outfielders, three relievers, a complete infield, and a five-man bench with two open DL spots.

His infield was solid, the Brown Mosquito thought. His pitching staff was strong. Not sure about these outfielders. The Mosquito looked over his team and imagined the possibilities.

The pimple-faced teenager behind the counter took the players' stacks of cards and added them up on a cash register.

"Pay now, or pay later?" the teenager asked Crazy Fool.

"Pay now," he said and handed over a hundred dollars. The teenager handed the cards back. "Good Luck," he said.

"Thanks," Crazy Fool said and made for the exit quickly. He wanted to manage his team on his own, away from the others, especially SF Tranny on Crak.

Waiting in line, SF Tranny looked up from her cards to see Crazy Fool, hurrying out the door.

Tranny couldn't stop the tear from welling unexpectedly. As she wiped it with her finger, careful not to smudge her makeup, SF Tranny thought, "It's not because someone I care about is running off on me... It's because I'm so happy for my beautiful butterfly, taking flight from his cocoon."

"Pay now, or pay later?" the teenager asked Team Rosebudd, who wore a helmet very much like Boba Fett.

Team Rosebudd's voice was synthesized behind the helmet. "Pay. Now." He handed over five $20's.

"WHHHHAAAARRRRRRRR," said the Newport Idiot.

Adam Horn stepped in to translate, "He said, 'Pay later.'"

The pimple-faced teenager pointed to a giant sign over the door:

Un-Paid League Fees will increase $10 each month from the date of the draft until paid.

The Idiot nodded and walked out of the store.

The Brown Mosquito laid a crisp Benjamin over the counter.

"Team Name?" the kid asked.

"The BROWN MOSQUITOS," he said. "In all-caps."

The kid typed it in and said, "Ok. Good Luck."

The Mosquito took his cards out into the bright sunlight. His players followed him out. He turned and faced his team. Ozzie was right. The magic was real. “I won't let you down,” he said, and his motivation became crystal clear. With this team of ballplayers, he would seek a standard of excellence, and create a legend all his own.

He took a deep breath and smelled the fresh breeze. Baseball was in the air.

Exposed

On a late day in late Spring, the Mosquito family was busy driving each other crazy. The brother Mosquito was fighting with sister Mosquito and Mama Mosquito was shouting at both of them over a bubbling pot of sauce.

The Brown Mosquito sat on the couch, trying to remain invisible and tune them out as he watched a baseball game on TV. His long nose dipped into a cocktail; Bombay Sapphire gimlet. He flipped through his baseball cards, pulling out Rich Harden, starting pitcher for the Cubs. He drafted him in the 11th round, and here he was, on the mound on TV.

The lights were on at Wrigley, which was still always strange to see, he thought, and the outfielders walked in place, slapping their gloves and getting ready for the next pitch.

Rich Harden was on the rubber, but something was out of place. They were in Wrigley Field, but the Cubs weren't playing. Rich Harden donned a white uniform, with yellow and brown stripes and the emblazoned "MOSQUITOS" scripted on the front of the jersey.

With one foot in the batter's box, big Ryan Howard took a huge practice cut. Behind him, Ryan Braun took a few swings in the on-deck circle. These two ballplayers had on black uniforms, with "CAPTAIN SHITBEARD" scripted in gold and red across their chests.

"Ryan Howard has had a great start to the season," the TV announcer said, "Seventeen homers already and he leads the league in RBI."

Howard pushed his pine-tar smeared helmet up above his eyes. You could barely make out the red and gold Shitbeard logo, a Buccaneer with an eye-patch and a frothy beard of shit.

The eyes of the pitcher were laser-focused, the hypodermic needle-nosed Brown Mosquito sewn onto his dusty brown ball cap. He pulled the glove over his head, lifted his leg high, and blazed a fastball that cut the plate and froze Howard.

"HEEEEEEET!" the umpire jabbed his arm out, ringing up Howard for strike three.

"Yes!" said the Brown Mosquito watching on his couch.

The score flashed on TV as the players headed for the dugout. The announcer concluded the inning, "We go to the break, with the score... Brown Mosquitos: 238, Captain Shitbeard, 172."

The Mosquito pumped one of his several fists and sucked in a long stingerful of gin.

"Babe? Babe? Can I get some help here?" Mama Mosquito was overwhelmed.

The Brown Mosquito bzzzzzzzzzzzzzz'd over.

"Can you chop these, and wash these, and also chop these?" she asked him.

Just as the Mosquito picked up the knife, she exclaimed, "Oh, no! I think I'm missing an ingredient!"

"Mama-mama-mama-mama-mama-mama-mama-mama-mama," the sister followed her around the kitchen as Mama Mosquito looked for the missing ingredient.

The brother Mosquito stomped in. "She hit me! She needs to have a consequence!" he shouted.

"Nut-uh," she rebutted.

"MAAAAaaaa! Maaaaaaaaaaa! Maaaaaaaaaaaa!!" they whined over and over.

"STOP IT!" Mama shouted. "I can't even think! I definitely don't have what I need. Babe, could you please, please, please go to the store for me?"

"Right now? It's gonna be packed," said the Brown Mosquito, who just wanted to watch the game and enjoy his cocktail.

"I'm sorry, I'll make it up to you," she kissed him on the cheek. "And while you're there... Let me make you a list. You wanna take the kids?"

"No, no, no, no, no," he said as he backed away to the door.

"I'll go, but not if he's going," sister said.

"Well I'm not going if she's going!" brother exploded back.

"No! No one's going. I'll be right back," the Mosquito inched closer to the door. "Just text me the list," he said and quickly departed before the raptor-like claws of the children got to him.

The Brown Mosquito walked out into the active city streets. The night was young and the air was brisk. As he whistled and walked to the store, something caught his eye. A newspaper stand.

The Brown Mosquito leaned over and picked up a paper.

The front-page headline could not be ignored:

KING OF POP DEAD

The Brown Mosquito flipped back to the sports section.

"I added up the fantasy calculations on paper, then typed it all up on my old Smith-Corona," the ghost voice of Ozzie Smith wafted in the night air. "Got all my stats from the newspaper."

The Brown Mosquito pulled out the sports section and scanned the headlines:

3 Home Runs By Adam Jones Win It For Cali Green

Verlander Strikes Out 13, SB Cherry Poppers Roll

Pujols Has Big Week For Happy HairyBalls

As he glanced up, he saw two men across the street. One had long dark hair, the other had short red curls, and they both wore business suits. They greeted each other and then gave each other the "Bash Brothers" forearm smack.

In a sudden FLASHBACK, the Brown Mosquito remembered being in a large stadium as two ballplayers met at home plate with the "Bash Brothers" forearm smack, celebrating a monster home run. The crowd was on their feet, creating a booming chamber of euphoria. The Brown Mosquito was there.

Those same two ballplayers were now in business suits and walked into an expensive hotel lobby together.

The Brown Mosquito ran across the street to try to catch up to them. He rubbed his sore wing, afraid to test it — when suddenly A TAXI HONKED and slammed on the brakes.

Halfway across the cars were going the other direction and the Brown Mosquito made a leap of faith.

"It's now or never," he said to himself and with a painful grimace and he engaged his wings. It was painful to fly but he summoned the strength to rise just over the oncoming cars. He caught an updraft and soared toward the closing lobby door.

Within an inch of closing, the Brown Mosquito spun sideways, and bZZZZZZZzzzzzzzzz'd through the lengthening rectangle of light just before it shut.

He flew over the heads of the two men in suits, and found a buttress on which to land. The hotel's lavish foyer had an abundance of nooks for a Mosquito to hide. He buzzed just over them, and tried to get a little closer to hear them talk.

"After the initial investment, there will be a slight downturn, but with expansion, profits will soar," the man with the long dark mullet was saying. "Got another big shipment coming into ESPN Headquarters this week."

"Just stick to the plan, José," the man with the curly orange hair said, "You start running your mouth again and you'll bring us all down."

The Mosquito now recognized him. It was Big Mac, from the billboard where they crashed the SB Cherry Popper. And the other must be José Canseco, Big Mac's Top Lieutenant.

The two men were huge, their tight suits barely containing them. Their bazooka-like arms and rock-shelf shoulders stretched the fabric as they walked. The Brown Mosquito bzzzzzzzz'd above at a safe distance.

"You get Price yet?" asked Big Mac.

"The price for steroids?" José asked.

"Shhhhhhh! Quiet you fool! You never know whose listening!" Big Mac quickly turned back and thought he saw something buzzing up in the golden chandelier.

"Not THE price! David Price!" McGwire shouted at him in a whisper. "Is he on board with the program?"

"Not yet. He's about as wholesome as there is. Wouldn't even take a bribe."

The Mosquito crept his six legs around the chandelier and saw them heading for a conference room.

"Stab him in the ass for all I care! We need the younger generation of players. Show them the benefits, how their numbers will soar! Once they see how big their stats can get — ahhhhhhh!"

His ear was bzzzzzzzz'd by the Brown Mosquito as he flew past him into the conference room.

The Mosquito landed on the ceiling and looked upside-down over the conference table at the men seated. They were all huge, every one of them. He realized he recognized some of them.

There was Alex Rodriguez. And over there, Sammy Sosa. And Roger Clemens. There was Rafael Palmeiro's mustache again, and Barry Bonds next to him. Ken Caminiti was across from Bonds, and the brothers Jason and Jeremy Giambi. Benito Santiago was also there, and Gary Sheffield, Manny Ramirez, and Andy Pettitte. All of them sat around talking and joking and flexing until José and Big Mac entered and quieted them.

"Why do we not have David PRICE!?" McGwire exclaimed.

"Well, we sent Alex down there, and we thought we won the kid over," said Benito.

"I took him to a strip club," said Manny. "Everything good that has happened to me has always been in a strip club."

The Mosquito buzzed to the other side of the ceiling for a better vantage.

"Roger had an order all lined up for him," offered Andy Pettitte. "But the kid refused it when Alex brought it to him in the clubhouse."

"Looks like another one slipped through the cracks," said Barry.

McGwire POUNDED the conference table with his huge fists and almost split it in two.

"NO one can slip through THE CRACK!!!!!!!" he shouted.

His face was burning red. His hair was on fire. His ears could torch at any second.

"We need EVERY young superstar on board with this!" he shouted. "Feed them the HGH, testosterone boosters, muscle gummies, gym candy, weight stackers, iron pumpers, and Arnold's! I want these players good and juiced before every single game!"

McGwire walked around the table — a menacing presence. "This will be our greatest legacy, gentleman.

Where we smash the record books and be remembered as the greatest generation to ever play the game."

"Oh, no," said the Brown Mosquito to himself. "I've got to warn the others. Fantasy baseball will be ruined! It'll be a complete farce if all the players are juicing."

He buzzed around looking for a way out. Some of the men started to notice the mosquito buzzing along the ceiling and walls.

There! An air vent across the room. As he bzzzzzzzzzzz'd towards it, the Brown Mosquito was suddenly SLAPPED by the shoe of Jason Giambi and CRASHED into the wall. He slid down to the floor in a stupor. Dazed, he looked up just in time to see a shoe coming down on top of him.

He spun away under the table, got to his feet and ran towards the sitting legs on the other side.

He bzzzzzzzzzzzzzzzzz'd to a shoe with an exposed spot of skin just above the ankle sock. The Mosquito landed on the expensive shoe and observed the skin and hair of the leg.

"AHHHHH!" Alex Rodriguez screamed like a little girl and grabbed his ankle.

The Brown Mosquito flew out from underneath, and Barry Bonds tried to swat him as he bzzzzzzzzzzzzz'd right past his big face.

The Brown Mosquito piloted himself like an F-14, in full control. He peeled back around towards the table.

"Alright," said the Brown Mosquito. "You wanna play rough? How 'bout we play dirty?"

He bzzzzzzzzzzzzzzzzzzzzzz'd the conference table and released a heavy trail of brown fog that clouded the men.

They coughed violently, keeling over. The Brown Mosquito lifted toward the ceiling over the brown cloud and bzzzzzzzzzzz'd through the air vent and disappeared, leaving the men confused and coughing and gasping for air.

Going Nowhere Fast

The Brown Mosquito raced through the city streets, buzzing back to full strength, using his expert piloting skills to dive and dodge through the chaos of the city.

He arrived at ESPN Headquarters, and the long flight of stairs they were all thrown down. It was now vacant except for an employee here and there.

“Great,” he sighed. “Where did they all go?”

The Mosquito searched the area for clues to his friends' disappearance and found blood on the stairs from where Adam Horn's head had been resting.

The Mosquito bzzzzzzzzz’d right to it and started slurping it up. “I’m starving,” he gasped and greedily soaked the blood in through his snout.

He bzzzzzzzzz’d around the steps looking for clues. Something caught his eye on the sidewalk. He flew to a large green bud on the ground. The Brown Mosquito picked it up and sniffed it.

"Cali Green," he said as he exhaled. "They must have gone this way."

The Mosquito raced up the street, buzzing past people as they waved him away from their bodies. Finally, at the end of three blocks, he found them. Well, not the other members of the league, exactly, but there she was. There was no mistaking her.

The sun streaked off the glistening hull of the SB CHERRY POPPER, held at bay by large landing feet, a sleek design built with ample space for cargo and pleasure excursions. The rocket boosters were in the stern, six of them. Enough throttle to jingle the panties off any of her occupants.

The ship sat vacant in an abandoned lot. The Brown Mosquito buzzed through the chain-link fence. No one was there.

"Hello?" he tried but no one answered.

The door was sealed shut. The Mosquito buzzed around and eventually found a little space in one of the vents to crawl through. He buzzed into the port side corridor and made his way to the cockpit. Nobody there.

He looked out the dusty windshield. Then he saw them. Running. Adam Horn was in the lead, shouting. The

Newport Idiot huffed behind, and all the others were sprinting toward the ship.

"Go, Go, Go!" Horn shouted at them, and then the Brown Mosquito heard the door opening. In a moment, Horn was right next to him, sweating and breathing heavily.

"Boy, I'm glad you're here," said Horn and he jumped into the cockpit chair.

"What is going on?" asked the Mosquito.

"No time to talk. We gotta get outta here," said Horn and he started warming up the ship. The Newport Idiot WAAAAAARRRRRRRFFFF'd and climbed aboard.

"Alright, Idiot, power up the thrusters and tap into the auxiliary in case we need it," said Horn. "I did my best to fix 'em but the connection is a little unstable."

"I need to tell you about Big Mac!" exclaimed the Brown Mosquito.

"Not now, kid," said Horn as he flipped switches. "We're about to be eaten for lunch if we don't get outta here."

Cali Green, Crazy Fool, and Captain Shitbeard all jumped on board, out of breath.

"Let's go! Let's go!" Horn shouted. "That 'thing' is right behind us!"

Coming into view through the windshield was TJ and SF Tranny on Crak — sprinting towards the ship.

"Come' on, come' on," said Horn.

"What are you running from?" asked the Brown Mosquito.

"That," Adam Horn answered.

Through the dusty haze of the windshield, a large shadow eclipsed the light.

"No. It can't be," the Mosquito stared.

"Oh, yeah. It is," said Horn and fired up the auxiliary power with a low hum. "And he is pissed off."

Wearing a Hawaiian shirt and khaki shorts that hugged his thighs like spandex, Jon, the restaurant manager, stomped after TJ and SF Tranny. The portly manager had swelled to enormous proportions, towering over three-story buildings. From deep in his bowels he let out an angry "ROAAAAAAAAR!"

The SB Cherry Popper started to lift off the ground. With long strides in a short skirt, SF Tranny pranced to the ship and leaped onto the rising door plank. TJ ran and jumped a little baby jump and barely got his hand up to the door. He held on for dear life as the ship rose off the ground. SF Tranny pulled him in and shut the door.

"They on?" Horn shouted. "Let's go." He pulled the ship towards vertical, rising over the monstrous blood-thirsty beast in a Hawaiian shirt.

“What the hell did you guys do to piss him off?” asked the Brown Mosquito.

“After about three or four too many Bear Fights, Captain Shitbeard started spraying ketchup dicks all over the restaurant,” said Horn. “On the walls, on the bar top, on the tables, on the super lame restaurant mural, all over the bar sinks, on the hostess stand, all over the kitchen, all over the computers, the TV’s, the dumbwaiter. There were red dicks everywhere.”

“How did he even find us here?” wondered the Mosquito.

Horn shrugged, looked at the Idiot, then back at Cali Green, Captain Shitbeard and Team Rosebudd, hidden behind his helmet.

They lifted above the city and Jon’s roars became more distant. Soon, the atmosphere became thin and the stars appeared.

“Let’s blow this popsicle stand,” Horn said cheerily, but then immediately became concerned as the power seemed strained and lights started blinking.

“Idiot are we on main thrusters?”

“WAAAAAAAAR.”

“Ok, switch ‘em over. I thought I made all the connections...”

The ship was having trouble speeding up.

“It’s not the thrusters,” said the Mosquito.

“They're pulling us in,” said Horn. “Some kind of tractor beam. Idiot, shut down all power. We're not going anywhere.”

The SB Cherry Popper was pulled stern-first back to the city of St. Louis.

“I told you that was too many ketchup dicks!” Crazy Fool shouted at Captain Shitbeard. “Who you think gotta clean that up?”

“I have a feeling this isn’t about the ketchup dicks,” said Horn. “That tractor beam is coming from ESPN Headquarters.”

A glowing purple beam emanating from a dish on the roof of ESPN pulled the SB Cherry Popper across the city.

“It’s Big Mac,” said the Brown Mosquito. “He and his henchmen are juicing up the players with steroids to increase their stats and break all the records.”

“Those bastards,” said Crazy Fool. “They’ll ruin fantasy baseball.”

“And they’re not going to let anything or anyone stand in their way,” said the Mosquito.

The ship was directed over Busch Stadium and it gently set her down in the outfield.

The crew looked out onto the field through the dusty windshield. The center fielder turned and looked up at them.

"Hey! It's Torii Hunter!" exclaimed SF Tranny on Crak. "He's on my team! Heeeey, Torii!"

Wearing the white, teal and pink of the SF Tranny on Crak uniform, Torii Hunter waved back.

The cabin door opened, and Adam Horn led the crew cautiously out into the sunlight.

He stepped onto the short, perfectly cut grass. The sun felt good on his face, and he looked around the ball park.

"Wow," was all he could say.

The others followed him out, TJ popping his fist in and out of his glove. The stadium was full of fans, but they were all completely quiet. A spaceship had just been deposited in centerfield.

"Going somewhere?" Mark McGwire boomed as he stepped out of the dugout, wearing his home St. Louis Cardinals uniform. "You take us for fools?"

The Brown Mosquito stepped forward. "We know what you're up to, and we're not going to let you get away with it."

"Ha," said McGwire. "And what is a little group of sissies going to do about it?"

Captain Shitbeard stepped forward and snarled.

"We're gonna beat the piss outta ya," Shitbeard said, "and then we're gonna shove those baseball bats up yar arse, each and every one of you."

Jason Giambi snarled, eager for a fight.

Barry Bonds BARKED like a dog.

Sammy Sosa slapped a bat over and over into his massive palm, attached to his massive forearm, and massive biceps.

The rest of McGwire's crew stepped out of the dugout, massive muscular beasts in their MLB uniforms.

"I own fantasy baseball," said Big Mac. "Which means I own you. So enjoy your little league and do what I tell you or I will rip apart your franchises and send you to the far reaches of the fantasy universe."

The Newport Idiot growled.

Captain Shitbeard spit.

Crazy Fool cracked his neck.

Adam Horn prepared to draw his blaster.

"How about we play for it?" TJ walked forward. "Winner takes over the league."

They all turned to him, stunned.

McGwire and his crew burst into laughter.

"You — want to play us?" McGwire asked, and his entire body started trembling in giggles. "In baseball?"

Canseco cracked up. Caminiti doubled over. A-Rod squeaked in a high-pitched girly laugh, and Manny Ramirez chuckled. The entire stadium erupted into contagious laughter.

The Mosquito looked at Horn, and then at Shitbeard. They weren't laughing.

"Head-to-head matchups," said the Brown Mosquito. "Your team against each of our teams. Strikeouts are worth 2."

McGwire laughed. "Fine. You're on. And when you lose, I am going to exterminate your league, and send each of you across the fantasy baseball universe to join already established leagues — full of strangers that you will never meet.

"No," said SF Tranny. "You wouldn't."

"I will," said Big Mac. "I will show you that you do not mess with me, or ESPN."

The Mosquito looked at the others. A small ragged group if there ever was one. But they had heart. They made it this far. And they were still standing.

"Batter up," McGwire smiled and returned to the dugout.

"I hope you're right about this," the Brown Mosquito said to TJ.

"Oh, he's right about this," said the Captain. "Let's go beat the piss out of these meatheads."

Jason Giambi flexed his muscles. Sammy Sosa sneered. Gary Sheffield spit a wad of dip juice that dripped down his chin.

Rafael Palmeiro's mustache widened in a smile, and he held up a dripping syringe. He quickly planted the needle into the ass of Andy Pettitte.

Pettitte's face slightly twitched, and as he felt the juice running through his veins his eyes widened. The power within him hardened his body like armor. His brow furled and he growled deep and animalistic.

HairyBalls Takes One for the Team

In the visiting team locker room, the Brown Mosquito pulled a brown sock high up to his knee. Then he went to the other five legs and pulled up five more stirrups. He took a deep breath and shook his head. "How are we going to pull this off?" he asked himself.

He looked around the locker room at his crew, his team, his battalion. They were either suiting up, stretching, or sitting at the bar drinking Mai Tai's.

Crazy Fool put on his spiked wrist bands.

SF Tranny was tying on her high-heeled cleats.

Happy HairyBalls shot pool by himself.

The Newport Idiot was roughly sewing two hats together to make one big hat to fit his giant head. His uniform of red lingerie left much to be desired.

"Here's to ya, Lappi!" shouted Captain Shitbeard as he raised his glass. His eyepatch was over one eye, to hide the bloodshot lazy eye he got when he was drunk.

"To the bitter end," the Captain shouted. "We shall fight to the bitter END!" He raised the glass higher and continued, "We shall fight this battle with honor! And if the end be near, may it be GLORIOUS!" he clinked glasses with Cali Green and slammed the shot of tequila.

"Fucking cheers, man," said Cali Green, taking his time with his shot of tequila. "We need to surf before you go, man."

"Daaaaaaaaaa," mumbled the Captain in his best Cosby impersonation.

"Go where?" TJ asked.

"Go our separate ways, man," said Cali Green. "You heard him. McGwire and his goon squad are gonna send us to the far reaches of the universe."

"But didn't you hear Captain Shitbeard?" TJ asked. "He said we're gonna fight. And the end would be glorious."

"He's drunk, man," Cali Green was stoned. "Look at him."

Shitbeard was crashed in a chair and singing, "If I get home before daylight, I just might get some sleep, ton-i-ight." His pirate hat slumped and his head dipped toward the open To-Go food containers all over the table in front of him.

As he started to pass out, his beard sank into the food of the open To-Go containers. Molecules of salsa found follicles of hair as the curled beard reached out into it. The salsa, the cheese, beans. The hairs curled into it all, absorbing nutrients. The food crawled into the beard, for protection. This symbiotic relationship continued on a regular cycle, anytime Captain Shitbeard passed out drunk into his open To-Go food containers.

"Come' on, TJ," said Adam Horn, putting on cowboy-boot-cleats. "We don't have a chance. These guys are Major Leaguers. They've hit hundreds – *thousands* – of home runs. You really think a team of space-traveling nitwits are going to get out of this alive? Hell, I'm not joining an established league with random strangers. Not me, kid. When I see my chance, I'm making a run for it."

"WAAAAARRRRRRRR," agreed the Newport Idiot.

"Yeah, real heroic, Horn," said Crazy Fool. "I knew we couldn't count on you. You run, coward!"

Horn tried to cross the room but he was stopped by the Idiot and others.

"I'm no coward!" Horn yelled back. "I'm a gambler! And I don't bet on losing hands!"

Crazy Fool stood up to confront him but was held back. The group shoved and pulled at each other until a LASER BLAST froze everyone.

"No one is making a run for it," Team Rosebudd announced, holding a smoking laser rifle.

The grips on each others' jerseys loosened and they all turned to face Rosebudd, shielded in body armor under his purple, green and gold baseball uniform. He wore a purple team hat with a single gold rose that sat on top of his face-masking Boba Fett-stlye helmet.

"You are all coming with me now," said Team Rosebudd.

"Why don't you take off your mask and show us what a traitor really looks like?" asked Horn.

"I am not a traitor, Adam Horn," said Rosebudd. "Like you, I am a gambler, placing my money on a winning hand."

Rosebudd took off his helmet to reveal a shaved head of smooth cappuccino skin.

"Christian Batista!" Horn exclaimed in shock. "But you're... dead!"

"I have been rebuilt, and retooled. And contracted to find you," said Batista.

"Listen," said Horn, "You tell Alvin the Hutt to eat a dick. He's nothing but a back-stabbing front-runner who thinks he knows more about sports than he actually does!"

"I am not here to bring you to Alvin," Batista said. "There is a much larger bounty on your head. And for the rest of you as well. Apparently, you have made some very powerful enemies."

"Ya? Who did we piss off this time?" asked Captain Shitbeard.

"The Baseball Writer's Association of America," Batista responded.

"WAAAR?" asked the Newport Idiot.

"The B-B-W-A-A," said Batista. "The organization who bestows baseball's MVP and CY Young awards, and votes on players eligible for the Hall of Fame. They are the protectors of baseball history and defenders of baseball's record book."

"What do they want with us, man?" asked Cali Green.

"You have caused a great disturbance in their institution. Certain statistics and baseball records have been called into question. The B-B-W-A-A does not want their reputation or the reputation of their heroic players tarnished by loud-mouth troublemakers like yourselves. Now, place these electronic handcuffs over your wrists and come with me — and no one will get hurt."

"Well, I guess we have no choice then," said Horn, ready to draw.

"Don't even try it, Horn," said Batista and raised his blaster at him.

The Brown Mosquito bzzzZZZZzzzzzz'd in Batista's ear, shaking him off target, and he blasted laser bolts into the walls and ceiling all around the locker room.

Horn and the others dove to the floor, flipping over tables and chairs for cover. Crazy Fool deflected blasts with his body board and took cover behind a foosball table.

Adam Horn hid behind a cement pylon and fired his blaster back at Batista.

Rosebudd flipped his helmet shield back down and took cover, firing his blaster back at Horn. Lasers rocketed across the room, exploding into the walls. Glass shattered above the bar. Plaster and cement crumbled down over the door to the hallway, sealing them in.

SF Tranny screamed and pranced for cover behind the pool table. Adam Horn fired back at Rosebudd. The two exchanged cross-fire as bright-colored BLASTS shot around the locker room.

Ducking behind a mound of broken slabs of concrete, the Brown Mosquito and Happy HairyBalls looked for a way out.

"What now?" HairyBalls asked him.

Glass liquor bottles on the bar shattered.

"Even if we get out of here we won't get very far as long as that tractor beam is still on," said the Brown Mosquito and looked around for another exit. Lasers blasts fired across the room. "We have to find a way to disable it."

"But how?" asked Hairy.

"It's coming from ESPN headquarters," said the Mosquito as he tried to think. "There has to be a way to jam the system."

"Jam the system? It's a pretty big system," said Hairy. "There are millions of stats a minute being pumped out of those computers." He poked his head out but then ducked again as laser blasts fired across the room.

"That's it, HairyBalls," said the Mosquito. "The stats! We'll need the biggest stats to jam the system and disable the tractor beam. And who has the biggest stats? The most home runs? The most strikeouts, wins, and saves?"

"McGwire's All-Star team," HairyBalls smiled.

"Their numbers are what give them their power," said the Brown Mosquito. "Without their stats, they're nothing."

Batista blasted the pylon protecting Adam Horn to a pulp and Horn had to abandon it. He dove and rolled across the floor to behind a couch.

"You'll never take us alive, Batista!" Horn shouted.

"It's our only hope," said the Brown Mosquito to Happy HairyBalls. "You go with the team and play in the game. Hold them off as long as you can while I sneak into the ESPN offices."

"No," said Hairy. "I'll go. I'll do it."

"It's too dangerous," said the Brown Mosquito. "I'll go. I'm smaller and can fit into tighter spaces."

"No. Let me," said Hairy. "This is my contribution to the league, to Satan's Bullpen."

The Brown Mosquito took notice of Happy HairyBalls, maybe for the first time. He was a good looking kid, young, his whole life in front of him. Days and days ahead of playing with his hairy balls. But the usual fun-loving guy was torn up inside. HairyBalls was moving toward fantasy football, like so many of them do. The Brown Mosquito had seen it coming.

"Give it up Horn!" shouted Rosebudd. "There is no escape!" He adjusted the scope of his rifle. He had the thinly protected Horn in his crosshairs.

"You know we can't come back for you," said the Brown Mosquito as he looked for an alternate exit. There was a door marked Player Exit on the far side.

"I know," said Hairy. "I have some family in Wisconsin and I plan on going up there and raising a family of my own."

"Well, alright, man," said the Mosquito and put one of his six arms on Happy's shoulder. "I'll never forget you. Someday they'll write stories of us and of your bravery today."

"I sure hope not," said Happy HairyBalls. He pulled down low the brim of his navy blue cap with a big orange "B." His jersey was the sleeveless navy Mike Ditka sweater but instead of BEARS, it said BALLS.

"I'll still be in for some March Madness if you'll have me," he said.

"Of course," said the Mosquito. "You can count on it."

Batista still had Horn in the crosshairs, but then he raised his rifle straight up and zeroed in on the light fixture directly above. He blasted it and it dropped onto Horn's head, knocking him out and the gun dropped from his hand.

The others put their hands up in surrender.

Happy HairyBalls reached into his pants and violently started tugging. The Mosquito started to worry as

HairyBalls grimaced and pulled and pulled deep inside his trousers. With a loud Riiiiiiip, he pulled out a fist-full of hair.

"Where do they keep the pine tar around here?" HairyBalls asked.

The visibility was thin with smoke and dust from the decimated walls. Rosebudd searched the room for survivors. He pulled back a large slab of concrete and found TJ and SF Tranny cowering over each other. Rosebudd attached the iron clasps to each of them and activated it with the remote on his belt. The metal bracelets clinked together, immobilizing them.

Rosebudd lined them all up against the wall; the Newport Idiot, Adam Horn, SF Tranny, Crazy Fool, TJ, Captain Shitbeard, and Cali Green. "Two more," he said and waved the rifle across the room in the dense fog. A rolling sound broke the silence, and then two objects appeared out of the mist, rolling towards him.

They stopped at his feet, and Rosebudd bent down to pick them up. He pulled back his helmet mask to get a better look.

He held them up — baseballs, smeared in pine tar and covered in short, curly hairs.

"There you go," said a voice in the fog. "Cradle them. Cradle my balls."

"Ewe!!!!" Rosebudd dropped the hairy balls and the rifle, completely grossed out. He tried to rub the pine tar off on his Team Rosebudd jersey, but he just got the curly hairs smeared all over it.

Out of nowhere, Happy HairyBalls tackled Rosebudd to the floor. The Mosquito buzzed in and landed on Rosebudd's utility belt. He pressed the RELEASE button on the remote and instantly freed the others as the metal braces dropped to the floor.

Captain Shitbeard grabbed Batista's arms from behind, and Cali Green slapped the cuffs on his wrists. The Mosquito flipped the remote back to SECURE and the braces clasped tight.

"You'll never get away with this!" Batista shouted.

SF Tranny picked up a hairy baseball and stuffed it in Rosebudd's mouth and then flipped the face shield back down. Rosebudd could only muffle his screams as he wiggled around on the ground.

Crazy Fool and the Newport Idiot pulled large slabs of concrete away from the door to clear an escape route to the tunnel.

Happy HairyBalls hurried to the door marked PLAYER EXIT. He looked back at them, one last time.

With everyone safely through into the tunnel, the Brown Mosquito turned back to Happy HairyBalls.

He gave the Mosquito a thumbs up. The Mosquito returned the gesture and then took off down the tunnel after the others.

They all ran down the underground tunnel, past stadium workers, mascots, and team executives, past the door leading to the Home Locker Room.

Beyond the door, large ballplayers stretched their uniforms over their ripped, muscular bodies; the brilliant bright clean colors of classic major league uniforms; the St. Louis Cardinals, the Chicago Cubs, the New York Yankees, the Los Angeles Dodgers. José Canseco waked around the locker room in a Texas Rangers uniform with a needle full of juice, asking if anyone needed another poke. Clemens raised his hand and José jabbed the needle into his ass cheek — right through his uniform.

Clemens groaned, then growled, his face turning red, angry, and violent. The players were all gearing up for a fight; flexing, roaring, and pounding their huge chests like gorillas.

The Matchup of the Century

On a cloudless summer day under a bright blue sky, the groundskeepers sprayed the Busch Stadium infield and outfield as the crowd started to file in.

The radiant green grass of the outfield sparkled in the hose water.

A little girl led her grandpa down the stairs by the hand. "Are we gonna see Big Mac hit a home run tonight, Grandpa?" she asked.

He eased his way down the steps and across the aisle ten rows behind the dugout. "I hope so, deary," he said. "I hope so." His red Cardinals hat was tilted high so he could watch his feet as they shimmied down the narrow row to his seat. "That Big Mac is something else. He could hit 80 home runs this year."

The grandpa looked up at the bright field. The infield was raked smooth, with dirt soft as a beach.

The Brown Mosquito was perched onto the padded rail of the dugout. His league-mates filed into the dugout around him.

The Mosquito smelled the fresh air with a deep breath, and took in the delightful sounds of the major league stadium. Cali Green popped next to him and stretched his arms. McGwire's All-Stars took the field to generous applause.

"What'd ya think, man?" Cali Green asked, watching the other team out on the field. "Singles and doubles? Stolen Bases and Runs?"

"No," said the Brown Mosquito. "If we want to beat them it'll be with pitching, and the long ball."

The Captain arrived on his other side. "Ya got the lineup, Skip?" Shitbeard asked.

"It's taped to the wall," replied the Mosquito without breaking his gaze at the All-Stars warming up.

On the dugout wall, a lineup card was posted. They all gathered around.

The lineup card was titled:

Satan's Bullpen

Final Regular Season Standings

2009

"Alright, listen up," Adam Horn said and read the card aloud. "Leading off and playing shortstop, with the best regular-season record of 17-5... is the Brown Mosquitos."

The players clapped. The Mosquito tipped his cap.

Horn went on, "The Brown Mosquitos receive $300 for winning the Pennant, and will have the number one seed in the first round of the playoffs."

The Mosquito pumped his many fists.

TJ wiggled in-between the larger men to try to see.

The Newport Idiot looked over heads, his red hat not looking quite right being split in half and sown together.

Captain Shitbeard took out a purple velvet pouch and slipped out a bottle of Crown Royal. He blinked and squinted and took a swig of the Crown as he tried to read the lineup card on the wall.

Horn continued, "With a 14-8 record, batting second and playing centerfield is... Crazy Fool."

Players clapped and Crazy Fool threw his bare arms up in the air, his Silver and Black uniform cut off at the sleeves.

"Batting 3rd and facing off against Crazy Fool in the first round of the playoffs is… Mesa T's."

TJ's smile grew across his plump cheeks and he turned red. He smiled wider and wider and a tear came to his eye. He then turned away, so the others wouldn't see him cry.

"Hitting cleanup, and in the final playoff spot to face the Brown Mosquitos are… are… "

Horn couldn't continue. He looked up at the Newport Idiot, who put a hand on his shoulder.

The Mosquito buzzed over, to see who he would be facing in the first round.

"The SB Cherry Poppers," the Brown Mosquito said and looked at Horn.

"We did it, kid. We really did it," said Horn.

"This isn't over yet," said the Brown Mosquitos. "The top four teams will face-off for two straight weeks in the first round of the playoffs, and the winners will face off for two straight weeks for the Championship."

"So the rest of us have nothing to play for?" asked the Newport Idiot.

The Mosquito shook his head. Heads sunk. Cali Green slapped his glove on the bench.

"The only way to do this is together," said the Brown Mosquito. "We've made it this far. And everything we ever wanted still stands right in front of us. Happy HairyBalls is on his way to disable the tractor beam. If we keep fighting, and give these guys everything we've got, we can hold them off long enough to get out of here with our league."

"And if we don't, HairyBalls risks himself for nothing," said Captain Shitbeard. "And we're not going to let each other down when our friends need us most."

Crazy Fool nodded.

"That's right!" said SF Tranny on Crak.

"So let's go out there and give it everything we've got!" said the Brown Mosquito. The others cheered and shouted. "And may the best team win!"

"Yeah!" they all shouted.

"Ladies and Gentlemen," the announcer's voice echoed. "Please welcome, Satan's Bullpen!"

The owners ran out onto the field and took their positions.

The sun was bright and the grass glistened. The players each wore a different uniform, but somehow they looked like a team as they tossed the ball around, warming up.

The Brown Mosquito and Adam Horn practiced scooping grounders on the left side of the infield and throwing them sharply to Captain Shitbeard at first base. The SNAP of Shitbeard's glove meant another one was coming as he whipped it around the infield.

There was a sudden stir in the outfield as the bleacher bums noticed someone coming out onto the field from the bullpen gate. It was none other than Tom Brady.

The announcer took over. "Here to throw out the first pitch, Multiple Super Bowl Champion... Tom Brady!"

The crowd went nuts. Mr. GQ jogged onto the field in his Patriots uniform wearing Ugg boots and an illuminating white smile that could fit in a horse's mouth.

There was a microphone waiting for him at the pitcher's mound. Brady eased up to it, trying not to get his Uggs dirty. He waved his fingers of sparkling Super Bowl rings to the adoring fans.

"I've never used steroids," he said into the microphone and they all quieted down, "but I sure do endorse cheating."

The crowd roared. Brady put both thumbs up and smiled. He waved back to them, his smile brighter than ever.

As the shadow of the grandstands moved onto the outfield grass, the umpire announced that it was time to "PLAY BALL!"

"Now batting, the Brown Mosquitos," the announcer boomed.

The Brown Mosquito bzzzzzzzz'd up to the plate. He took a few practice cuts. Even though his wooden bat was too big for his minuscule size, to Benito Santiago from behind his catching mask it looked like a toothpick. The catcher chuckled and wondered how that little thing was gonna hit the much bigger baseball.

The Mosquito dug in, grinding his back legs into the dirt. He waved the bat above him and stared down the pitcher.

Roger Clemens, "The Rocket," looked down from the pitcher's mound at his impossibly small target. "You want me to roll it in?" he asked, and his teammates laughed.

The Mosquito said nothing, but stared back and tried to focus. He had made some good moves during the season. Jason Kubel had 28 HR's that year, and over 100 RBI. Brad Hawpe and Luke Scott provided extra power in the outfield, each with over 20 homers. But it was second-round pick Chase Utley with 31 HR's and a shrewd mid-season pickup of Troy Tulowitzki with 32 homers that anchored his power game. If only he could harness some of that power against The Rocket right here.

The power pitcher blew a fastball by him that kicked up a sand storm and blew the Mosquito way back to the backstop.

The Brown Mosquito shook his head and spit out dirt and tried to regain his equilibrium. He bzzzzzzzzzz'd his wings free of dust and dirt.

Clemens laughed, caught the ball from Santiago and walked back up the mound.

The Mosquito dusted himself off and got ready to get back in there.

"Bonsai!" Someone shouted from the crowd.

The Brown Mosquito looked up. A fan held up a shot glass with green liquid fire in it.

The Mosquito walked over and bowed to him with his palms together. He took the glass from the fan and drank the green Bonsai Pipeline shot in one smooth take. Then he held on as the green wave of the Bonsai Pipeline rose over him. Keeping his balance, the Brown Mosquito surfed the surge of adrenaline, the blood rushing through his head. He held on as the barreling wave threatened to throw him off, but he kept his line and was thrust out the other side, feeling the ocean spray behind him as he rode the wave safely out.

"BONSAI!" the Mosquito shouted to the fan, and again bowed with both hands together.

The Brown Mosquito got back in the box, his eyes glowing green.

The Rocket reared back and fired. The Brown Mosquito swung and missed with such force that he spun around and around like a tornado as the force of the pitch again blew him back.

"STEEEEEE— RIKE TWO!" shouted the umpire.

The Brown Mosquito looked into the dugout. They were all up on the rail. Cali Green, Captain Shitbeard, the Newport Idiot.

"You got this Mosquitos," clapped Adam Horn.

"Here we go, here we go," Captain Shitbeard chanted as he paced.

"You got this motha fucka!" shouted Crazy Fool.

The Mosquito stared down Clemens' glove, focused on the pearl hidden inside. Clemens kicked back, and as his arm came forward, the pearl appeared. Very quickly the Mosquito saw that the ball was spinning. It was a slider. "Go the other way," he heard Ozzie in his ear.

The Mosquito's large bug-eyes followed the spinning ball as it tailed away from him and when it was time he met it with his bat, in a light chop designed to go to the opposite field. He connected perfectly and drove the ball the other way into right.

The Brown Mosquito bzzzzzzzz'd down to first base and made the turn as Barry Bonds got the ball back in from the outfield.

On the scoreboard, the number 1 lit up under HIT, and the BROWN MOSQUITOS score changed from 0 to 1.

"Alright!" the dugout shouted."Here we go!"

Crazy Fool was up next. He stepped in with his cut-off sleeves and studded bracelets. He waved his bat around and got ready for the pitch.

The Brown Mosquito danced off first, held on by Jason Giambi.

Above in the sky, the Brown Mosquito saw the purplish tractor beam pull in another fantasy league.

He started wondering about Happy HairyBalls. If he doesn't make it into ESPN and switch off that tractor beam, the Mosquito thought, this whole plan was doomed.

"Come' on, Crazy Fool!" shouted SF Tranny. "Show 'em what you got!"

Clemens whirled and threw, catching the Brown Mosquito off-guard. He dove back but he knew it was too late. The glove slapped his arm as it reached for the bag.

"YEEEEE— OUT!" shouted the umpire.

The crowd cheered. The Mosquito spit dirt out of his mouth and picked himself up off the infield.

The announcer stated, "Caught Stealing, Negative One."

The Brown Mosquito's score went from 1 back to 0.

Clemens laughed as he got the ball back.

The Brown Mosquito indignantly jogged back to the dugout to "Booooo's."

"Come' on, Happy HairyBalls," he thought. "We need to buy him some time."

Above in the sky the tractor beam pulled in another ship.

Boomer Blows Up

Happy HairyBalls ducked behind some bushes as a security guard walked past. He peeked up over the top of the leaves at the shoebox-shaped ESPN building protected behind a thickly barred fence.

He ducked again as another ESPN security guard walked by. HairyBalls trudged through the shrubs, trying to make as little noise as possible. He circled the fence to the back of the building where a delivery truck backed into the loading dock area.

A stout balding man was directing the driver with his arms. "Back, back, back, back, back, back," he said as he waved his arms towards himself.

"It's Chris Berman!" Happy HairyBalls said out loud. A guard turned and Hairy ducked into the bushes and put his hand over his mouth. He quietly pulled back the branches to see.

SportsCenter anchor Chris Berman held both palms out and the truck came to a stop. Other ESPN workers arrived to help unload the truck.

"Let's go! We don't have all day here," Chris Berman shouted at the crew.

"You Berman?" the driver held out a clipboard.

"Yeah," Berman said as he signed the paperwork.

"Like, *the* Chris Berman? Like, you know — Boomer?"

"Yeah. That's me," said the stout bald man.

"Awe, love your stuff, man. Chuck New-Kids-on-Knoblauch? John I-am-not-a-Kruk?"

"Yeah, yeah. That's me," Berman said as he signed sheet after sheet on the clipboard.

The driver motioned to the boxes being unloaded with FRAGILE stamped on all of them. "What is all this stuff, anyway?" he asked. "New hair product or something?"

Forklifts rolled in to carry off tall stacks of boxes into the warehouse.

"Ha, you're funny," said Berman. "Just be careful with that stuff. Something for the boss. I don't ask questions." Berman handed him back the clipboard.

The driver smiled. "I can't believe in standing here with *the* Chris Berman. I'm your biggest fan. Love your nicknames. What's your favorite sports nickname?"

"I don't have one," Berman said as if rehearsed a million times. He turned to the forklifts. "Careful with that!" he shouted.

"Come'on," said the driver. "Just one?"

"It'd be like trying to pick your favorite child," said Boomer. "Let's go! Careful!" he shouted to the crew. And then because Berman couldn't help talking about himself, he said, "Alright. I maybe have one or two favorites."

"Awe, man. You are the best," the driver gushed.

Happy HairyBalls saw it as a chance to sneak through the gate and across the lot. He hid behind the large tire of the 18-wheeler and looked out. There was a security guard by the back door and there were employees all over the loading dock.

"Great," thought Hairy. "How am I gonna get in there?"

Berman reminisced, "My favorite name brings up an air of the forgotten days of youth, as Oddibe 'Young Again' McDowell, always professed. And there was a time in the 60's when Von 'Purple' Hayes was very popular."

"I always liked Mike 'Lego My Gallego," said the driver.

They laughed.

"You remember Todd Snap Crackle Van Popple? Or how about Todd Highway to Helton?" asked Berman. "Or what about Delino 'Decoconut' Deshields? Lance You Sunk My Blankenship!"

The driver doubled over in laughter. "Stop! Stop it!"

Hairy crept behind a stack of empty crates, right below the loading dock.

A pale ESPN worker in a hard hat laughed and leaned against the wall. Berman kept going and the employee kept laughing, and as he leaned back against the wall his shoulder pushed a big red button that started to lower the heavy warehouse doors.

"Bert Be Home Blyleven?" Berman laughed. "Mike Nova Scioscia?"

"Stop, man, you're killing me!"

Hairy peeked out. The guard's back was to him. He saw his chance. He bolted for the back door but right in the middle of the lot he FROZE when heard:

"STOP!" Then, "NOOOOOOOOOO!"

Happy's hairy balls were frozen, completely exposed in the middle of the lot. He turned to the warehouse.

The big loading dock door came down just as a forklift carrying a tall stack of boxes was underneath it. The heavy door CRUSHED the boxes one by one, exploding the contents within. Glass shattered and brown liquid splattered.

Another forklift going too fast CRASHED into that one and the tall stack of boxes wobbled and wobbled and fell, the glass tubes inside shattered, and brown liquid oozed out all over the loading dock.

The warehouse door dropped all the way down to the ground, pulverizing the boxes.

The security guard by the door was distracted by the commotion. A security camera above recorded the scene on the loading dock, and Berman's rant.

Chris Berman's face turned BEAT RED. He put up his index finger, shook his head to the right, waved his finger right-left-right-left, and exploded into a tirade.

"When I'm doing TV and I got 18…" Berman started, but someone frantically tried to catch a box from another wobbling stack — but it fell and broke.

"God Damn it. Can't everybody stop for ten minutes?" He continued, "I mean everybody seems that that's the only time...Everybody can we... Jesus Christ. I mean it's not that much to ask."

The security guard by the back door abandoned his post to help clean up the mess. Happy HairyBalls snuck below him.

"Is that when everybody has to move?" Berman went on. "When I'm trying to concentrate? Jesus."

The driver leaned over a crew member, "And you guys thought I was a pain in the ass."

Berman continued his tirade. "I mean that's so rude, I can't believe that that's that... that's so God Damn rude. Just, why does everyone all of sudden have to move? You've had two fucking hours to move around. Wait ten minutes. Jesus."

Boomer put his hand to his forehead, so completely distraught. He casually picked his nose and asked, "I'm sorry to explode like that but that's, it's like no one's ever worked on TV here before? Jesus."

He paused for a moment, still fuming. The crew cleaned up and tried to ignore him. Berman quickly picked his nose again and continued, "Saw a kid under the... What the FUCK do they think I'm doing? I, I really, I actually can't believe what I just saw. It's like no one here has worked on TV before. If I hear a dial-tone."

He took a sip of Diet Coke and then brings it home, "And there were 7 people th— I mean, Jesus. We need to use the studio for 15 FUCKING minutes, just everybody, you know..." He put his hand back over his forehead and pouted.

He went in for another pick, smelled it, is about to eat it when…

Happy HairyBalls slipped in through the back door into ESPN Headquarters and the door shut behind him.

Above the door was a sign:

ESPN HEADQUARTERS
Bristol, Connecticut.

High up on the corner of the building the security camera blinked red, recording Berman's entire outburst.

Several days later, one of the forklift crew-members obtained the footage and leaked it to the internet. This tirade can be viewed word-for-word in its' entirety by going to youtube.com and searching "Chris Berman Crazy Rant."

Dingers

The door slammed shut and Happy HairyBalls scurried through the hallways of ESPN Headquarters with his head down, trying to stay unnoticed. He came to a room full of cubicles and he snuck quickly through the maze of desks. In one of the cubicles, he had to carefully creep behind the large throne of a king, with LeBron James sitting in it on a phone call.

In the hallways, NFL, NCAA, NBA, MLB, and NHL mascots walked to and from offices, as well as executives, anchors, and professional sports stars in their full uniforms. No one seemed to notice Happy HairyBalls, at least not yet.

"What would Ditka do? What would Ditka do? What would Ditka do?" the Wisconsin native and serious Bears fan nervously asked himself as he looked around the offices.

He got to a side hallway and crept along the wall. He could hear heavy machinery on the other side of the wall but he couldn't tell what it was. He could sense it was a big, hollow, cavernous room with many echoing clinks and clanks. Ahead were two heavy doors with chemical warning signs plastered all over them. He approached doors but they suddenly opened and HairyBalls had to duck away.

Two scientists exited and stood outside the door, chatting. Happy HairyBalls quickly found an unlocked door and disappeared. He found himself in a pitch black closet.

Listening for the men to pass in the hall, HairyBalls turned his attention to finding a light in the dark. He felt fuzzy things all around that grazed his skin like feathers.

"What is this place?" he wondered. "This better not be one of SF Tranny's dumpsters," he thought.

He finally found a light on a string that illuminated the room. He was in the mascot dressing room, surrounded by the costumes of Tigers and Bears and Huskies and Cougars, and all the other mascots of the world of sports. Here was San Diego's "Swinging Friar" costume, and "Lou Seal," from San Francisco.

He heard someone opening the door.

A large, bobble-headed man with a long blonde curled-up mustache entered and sat on a bench, done with his shift for the day. Bernie Brewer started to take off his

Brewers jersey when he heard someone in the dressing room, hiding in the racks of costumes.

His large wobbly eyes searched the racks. He flipped through the hundreds of wardrobes. Suddenly a purple face popped out at him, a dinosaur, with a white horn on his snout, and two more horns on the top of his head on either side of a Colorado Rockies hat.

Bernie Brewer waved, embarrassed, which he expressed by making all kinds of mascot gestures.

Dinger, the purple dinosaur mascot, waved back in a "no big deal" gesture.

Inside the costume, a sweaty Happy HairyBalls scooted himself past Bernie Brewer and made his way out of the racks of clothes, his purple tail following. On his way to the door he checked his costume in the big mirror and straightened his Rockies jersey and hat.

Opening the dressing room door, Dinger the dinosaur looked around and then walked confidently down the hall back to the big heavy doors with chemical warnings. He pulled them open and entered the large laboratory.

The interior was huge, bigger than an airplane hanger. Enormous glass vats you could drive a car through were suspended by thick cables from the ceiling. Inside each of the vats there was a bubbling brown liquid.

"Hey, you there!" a voice stopped Dinger in his tracks. "You aren't supposed to be down here!" A lab assistant approached him.

Dinger put his palms up, tapped his forehead with his mitt and shook his head.

"Alright, it's alright," said the assistant. He pointed him in the right direction. "Go over that gang-plank there to the door on the other side. That'll bring you back to the offices."

Dinger the dinosaur thrust his hands out, then clasped them over his chest, and then reached out and gave the lab assistant a great big mascot hug.

"Ok, ok," the lab tech said. "That's ok."

Dinger wobbled over the gang-plank in-between massive glass vats and then turned and waved back. He walked to the door and opened it, a red light flicked on above him.

From across the room, the lab assistant saw the red light, and then when it changed back to green, he went back to work.

HairyBalls watched him leave, hidden behind the vat. He proceeded to investigate the room in the purple dinosaur costume, stepping over pipes, making his way around large equipment.

"This must be what's powering the tractor beam," he thought as he explored.

The vats and vessels and pipes all led to a single output station. The result of all this chemical engineering was fed into three large black tubes connected to a supercomputer.

The supercomputer was shaped like a 60-ton black brick, with lights blinking throughout. Happy HairyBalls took off the dinosaur helmet to get a closer look.

Individual wires connected to different panels, and some were labeled. In fact, some were labeled with the names of baseball players.

Wires crossed into a circuit board with red digital numerals displaying the players' current statistics:

Manny Ramirez: 555 HR's, 2,574 Hits.
Alex Rodriguez: 696 HR's, 2086 RBI.
Barry Bonds: 762 HR's, 2,935 Hits, 1996 RBI.

He looked back at all the clear vials of brown liquid feeding into this machine.

"They're juicing the stats!" Hairy realized.

He looked up at the high ceiling of the massive room. Bright outside light poured in through large glass-paneled skylights in a hexagon pattern at the center of the ceiling. Posted on the roof outside was the huge satellite dish of the tractor beam.

"This is it!" exclaimed Hairy. "I need to erase all these stats that are powering the tractor beam!"

"Erase all the stats?" a voice behind him said. It was a man in a cheap suit with three imposing mascot escorts; Ace – the Toronto Blue Jay, the Philly Phanatic, and Wally the Green Monster.

"You think you can just *erase* baseball stats?" the man stared him down. "These numbers are our history."

"Who are you?" asked Happy HairyBalls.

"I am the Director of the Baseball's Writer's Association of America," he said. "The B-B-W-A-A."

"Then you need to know these stats are inflated!" exclaimed Hairy. "They should be erased for all of eternity!"

"That is not for you to decide," the man said. "You see, we like big numbers in baseball. We're in a struggling ratings market with much lower revenue than the big boys at the NFL and NBA. We need to forge our place into society's hearts, and wallets, and we do that by creating a product that excites them. And nothing excites the fans more than Home Runs."

He walked over to the computer terminal and turned on several screens. Holding the Dinger dinosaur mask, Hairy followed him, pushed along by the three mascots. Ace the Blue Jay ripped the Dinger mask out of Hairy's hands and shook his head in stern disappointment.

"Ah, looks like Rafael Palmeiro is up," the man in the cheap suit said as he leaned over the controls. "Let's give him a little boost, shall we?"

On the screen, the game was being played between Satan's Bullpen and Mark McGwire's MLB All-Stars. Cali Green was smoothing the dirt in front of the mound with the toe of his cleat. He leaned into the stretch for the sign.

At the plate, Rafael Palmeiro took a practice cut and pulled back into his batting stance.

The man in the cheap suit flipped some switches and powered up a lever. On a computer panel next to the broadcast of the game, Palmeiro's statistics were displayed:

Rafael Palmeiro:
Hits: 3,019
Home Runs: 568
RBI: 1833.

The man in the suit clicked two switches once and a third twice and the numbers on the board changed:

Hits: 3,020
Home Runs: 569
RBI: 1835

Hairy looked at him, puzzled. Through the hexagon of glass panels on the ceiling above, the satellite was switched on and a glowing beam of purple light was cast.

On the broadcast monitor, Cali Green checked the runner at second, then went into his leg kick and fired a pitch.

Palmeiro turned on it and CRUSHED it a mile.

The outfielders turned and watched it leave the yard.

"You just created a two-run dinger," said Happy HairyBalls, amazed.

The Director of the BBWAA smiled. "Look at them," he said and pointed to the screen.

A different angle replay showed Palmeiro crushing the ball and the ecstatic reaction of fans as the ball blasted off his bat and into the sky.

"They love it," the man smiled.

The TV broadcast flashed the score:

McGwire's All-Stars:	449
1. Brown Mosquitos:	241
4. SB Cherry Poppers:	229
2. Crazy Fool:	224
3. Mesa T's:	195

"No! You can't do this!" You're cheating the fans!" exclaimed HairyBalls. "You have to shut it down! You're destroying everything great about this game! It's all a lie!"

"Take him away," the man in the cheap suit had heard enough. The mascots grabbed Happy by his hairy balls.

"You're the Baseball Writer's Association of America!" HairyBalls shouted. "You have to speak up! The people will listen to you! Please! Fantasy Baseball will never survive!"

"Oh, fantasy baseball will survive," said the Director. "It will flourish, with statistics you never thought possible, giving us records that are broken game after game, season after season! The writers will provide spellbinding stories for the public to embrace as we celebrate new milestones, and sports fans will finally return their love and bring passion back to America's greatest pastime."

He mumbled an evil laugh, which turned excited at the possibilities in his mind.

"You'll never get away with this!" shouted Hairy.

"Take him to the roof," said the man in the cheap suit. "See if dinosaurs can fly."

The mascots dragged him away, kicking and screaming.

The Brown Mosquitos Get Some Help

"*Now batting,*" the stadium announcer boomed out the loudspeakers. "Gary Sheffield."

The behemoth ballplayer in his Los Angeles Dodgers uniform stepped into the batter's box. He spit a wad of tobacco that splattered across the white plate . His eyes were forged in fire as he stared down the pitcher. He spit again and the dip juice dripped down his chin.

Over the webbing of his glove and under the low-drawn bill of his ball cap, the eyes of Cali Green stared darts into the strike zone.

Crouched behind the plate, SF Tranny flashed a single skinny finger from his/her nether regions. Fastball.

Cali Green inhaled the leather of his glove. His two fingers felt around the seams of the baseball as he turned it into the grip he wanted.

He kicked and delivered, smoking a 92 mph fastball down the inside part of the plate. It was turned around with a WHACK from the bat of Sheffield. In the deafening silence, Sheffield smirked and tossed the bat, then started to lightly jog around the bases. The ball sailed on and on and on. It eventually disappeared into the upper concourse and fans scrambled to claim it. The crowd ROARED.

Sheffield snarled at Cali Green as he jaunted around the bases. The scoreboard added six more points.

Cali Green's mouth hung wide open. Suddenly the Brown Mosquito was bzzzzzzzzing into it, filling Cali Green's mouth with brown flatulence.

"Ahhhhhh!" he complained, shaking around on the pitcher's mound and finally spitting out the Brown Mosquito.

"Wake up!" the Mosquito shouted at him. "We need to use our heads! What they have in muscle, they lack in brainpower. We need to out-smart them."

"Alright, man," Cali Green wobbled back up the hill. "Thanks for the pep talk, man." He spit. "Nothing worse than a Brown Mosquito in your mouth."

The Mosquito buzzed back to short and got in a ready position.

"Now batting, Alex Rodriguez," the announcer boomed and the hulking beast walked to the plate. He wore Yankee Navy pinstripes. His arms were the size of tank cannons. His neck could swallow a gator. The batting helmet creaked as the head inside threatened to crack it wide open.

He took a practice swing with half the trunk of a tree.

Cali Green hid behind his glove, only his eyes appearing ninja-like.

A-Rod's face gushed sweat as his body prepared to explode at the pitch.

Cali Green's eyes slowly started to turn red as lightning bolt-shaped rivers of blood darted through them. Smoke rose from the glove.

"There we go, Cali Green!" Crazy Fool shouted from centerfield.

The smoke cloud grew until you couldn't see Cali's face, and then he went into his windup.

He kicked his skinny leg high, his knee shooting over his head, and came down with a joint in his mouth and a nasty twist of the wrist.

As soon as the ball left his hand, the baseball began spinning and twirling in loops, a feat of centrifugal force unthinkable. Around and around it twirled like a loop-de-loop rollercoaster that never stopped.

A-Rod loaded up, the pitch taking an impossibly long time to reach him.

The Mosquito pumped his glove at short.

A-Rod took a huge cut and WHIFFED. The crowd felt the breeze of the giant swing as the Goliath crashed to one knee.

"STEEEEEEEEEERIKE ONE!" the umpire shouted.

Adam Horn relaxed at third and got ready for the next pitch. "There we go, Cali. Give him the Green."

The Mosquito got low, ready to smack his glove on the ground if it came to him. A faint light appeared beside him, crouched in the same ready position.

"Ozzie," the Mosquito said to the hologram-like figure.

"Yeah, buddy. Here we go, here we go," Ozzie was smiling as bright as the sun. "Where would you rather be?" He slapped his glove as Cali Green kicked and delivered.

The ball this time took a huge trajectory, high out to the left, then rode like a wave back to the other side in a sweeping motion, then swept back to the left and then it finally darted back over the plate.

A-Rod was a little anxious and barely got a piece, driving it into the ground to the left side of the infield. The Brown Mosquito bzzzzzzzzzz'd into action, scooping up the ball and throwing it to Shitbeard at first to easily get A-Rod running down the line.

A few in the crowd clapped. Some held up signs. Others barely looked up.

"Nice, man!" Ozzie said. "Where'd you get those moves?"

"Think I was just born with 'em," said the Brown Mosquito.

"Maybe," said Ozzie. "May be. Or maybe you've seen the magic."

The next pitch was popped high up in the infield, so high that everyone lost sight of it.

The batter, Manny Ramirez, looked up into the sky for it and jogged lightly to first.

"All I know is if we don't beat these guys, there will be no magic," said the Brown Mosquito, looking for the ball.

All the players were trying to find it, waiting for any sign of the massive pop-up, miles overhead.

Ozzie looked from the sky back to the Brown Mosquito, sizing him up and down. "Well, then," he said, "I guess you are ready."

The Brown Mosquito turned back to him but Ozzie was gone and someone else was in his place. The ballplayer lightly slapped his hand in his glove and looked up for the ball.

"Who are you?" asked the Brown Mosquito.

"Carlos Correa. Houston Astros. You won't pick me up until 2015 when I come up from the minors. It was a good pick. I helped you win the Timmy that year."

"The Timmy?"

"Yeah, your trophy. Our trophy."

"So, I'll win the Championship in 2015?"

"Dude, the Brown Mosquitos won four Championships in ten years. And are still going for more. Multiple Pennants, high-scoring records. The Brown Mosquitos are the class of the league. All of us want to play for you guys."

Correa located the falling baseball and moved into position towards the mound. He followed the ball the whole way until it arrived with a re-entry sizzle into his glove.

The crowd cheered. Correa whipped it around the horn.

"Now batting, Sammy Sosa," the player is announced and the beast stomped into the batter's box.

Cali Green's eyes were completely red now with little dots of white bouncing around like tadpoles. "Ok, man," he said, "Here comes the Seattle Supersonic."

He twirled his body and jumped away from the plate.

Players dove out of the way as the ball rocketed toward the dugout, DINGED off the rail, blasted back across the stadium, BINGED off a railing in section 528 and ping-ponged around the stadium. It blasted through a huge bucket of popcorn being eaten by a chubby man named Ian.

"Sammy Sosa!" said Ian and shoved the last of the popcorn into his mouth.

The ball flew back and forth across the stadium, but Sosa kept both eyes on it as it zipped around and around. It smacked into a giant beer advertisement that wobbled on impact and whipped it back toward home plate. The effect trampolined it back at incredible speed, the ball gaining a warm glow and small flames.

Sosa watched it come toward him and he WHACKED it with his mighty lumber.

All eyes turned skyward as the ball sailed high above.

Outfielder George Springer raced to the wall, watching the ball the whole way. In an incredibly athletic feat, he ran up the wall and reached over to snatch it out of the air just before it left the yard.

The crowd ROARED as he held up the ball in his glove.

"That's my boy!" Carlos Correa shouted and pointed to him. "That's my boy Springer!"

"Nice catch, baby!" Correa shouted as they ran into the dugout and high-fived. Then to the Mosquito, Correa said, "You were the first in the league to pick him up in 2014. And then you brought him back in '16. We had a good squad that year. Anthony Rizzo at first, Trea Turner and myself up the middle, Nolan Arenado at third."

They reached the dugout and the Brown Mosquito grabbed a bat and a helmet from the rack.

"Springer hit 29 HR's that year for the Brown Mosquitos," continued Correa. "We had Yoenis Céspedes. He hit 31. Rizzo had 32. Arenado had 41."

"So I was right," said the Brown Mosquito as he put his brown batting helmet with the yellow Mosquito logo onto his small head. "We have to beat them with power."

"Now batting, the Brown Mosquitos," the stadium voice booms.

"Not always," said Correa. "You've won quite a few Championships with impressive starting pitching, too. The Brown Mosquitos always seem to find a way."

The Mosquito buzzed up the dugout stairs with his bat but someone bumped into him from behind. "Sorry, skip," said the ballplayer in a Brown Mosquito uniform. "I'm up."

"Nolan Arenado?"

"Yeah," he said. "I think it's about time we give these guys a little taste of their own medicine. We're here for ya, skip. Let's go win this thing."

The Brown Mosquito looked into the dugout at all the major league ballplayers he drafted. George Springer put his arm on the shoulder of Anthony Rizzo. Yoenis Céspedes nodded. Tim Lincecum gave him the thumbs up.

"Oh, and skip?" Nolan turned back to the Brown Mosquito as he put on his brown helmet, "Everyone in that dugout plays ball the right way. No needle is ever touching my ass."

Arenado saluted him by touching the tip of his bat to the brim of his Mosquito helmet and he walked to the batter's box. Roger Clemens was done warming up and was breathing fire.

The Mosquito watched from the dugout as Arenado rhythmically waved his bat and then settled into his stance.

The hulking Rocket reared back and fired his blazing fastball, to which Nolan connected with a CRACK!

All Day

Happy HairyBalls was marched down the corridors of ESPN Headquarters, the three mascots holding him tight and keeping a close eye on him. The Philly Phanatic had the tightest grip as he pulled Hairy along. Many sports celebrities passed them in the halls and plenty of other mascots, all going about the business of a normal day at ESPN Headquarters.

Brutus Buckeye walked by with his giant melon-shaped head, flipping through a binder titled "Michigan Playbook."

Peyton Manning in shoulder pads and Colts uniform talked with Kevin Durant in his Oklahoma City jersey.

Otto the Syracuse Orange filled up a glass of orange juice at the employee snack and coffee stand.

Happy HairyBalls winced as he was roughly forced onward.

"Can't we *talk* about this?" Ace smacked the back of his head. "Oh, that's right," said Hairy. "You *can't* talk."

Up ahead, the St. Louis Cardinal mascot Fredbird wasn't watching where he was going and crashed into Clark, the Chicago Cubs mascot, who spilled his notes everywhere.

Clark was furious and shoved Fredbird. Fredbird shoved him back and then Clark smacked him in the head. Fredbird swatted back and the two exchanged heated blows with soft heavy mitts.

Other mascots tried to get in to break it up but a water cooler was knocked over and they really started going at it, a fury propelled by years of built-up hatred from their teams' often intense rivalry.

More people and mascots arrived to see the commotion. The hallway was getting crowded.

"Psst! Hey!" Hairy heard someone whisper. "Over here!"

A man in a purple football jersey motioned to him.

"Adrian Peterson?" Hairy asked.

"This way!" A.P. motioned to an adjoining office.

The mascots were all distracted as the fight raged on, knocking over potted plants, picture frames.

HairyBalls jerked away from Ace's clasp and darted after Peterson. Ace tried to grab him but he was cut off by the slow-moving crowd cheering on the fight. Ace pushed through them to try to get after Happy HairyBalls.

HairyBalls ran after number 28 up ahead, through the maze of hallways throughout the building.

"Slow down, man," panted Hairy. "I can't keep up."

Peterson hadn't even broken a sweat. "Oh, man. This is as slow as I can go."

A.P. juked an oncoming camera-man, side-hopped to avoid two production assistants, and put a textbook spin around SportsCenter anchor Linda Cohn. Her hair whooshed as he blew by her.

"Wait! I can't do that!" shouted Hairy. He tried to keep up, bumping into the production assistants and the cameraman and then spun around Linda Cohn.

Finally, Peterson stopped. "Touchdown," he said.

Hairy bent over both knees and gasped for breath. When he was finally able to lift his head, he read the sign above the door: ESPN FANTASY FOOTBALL.

They walked inside the large room filled with a buzz of activity, much like the Fantasy Baseball Offices, but the room was dark, and all the screens illuminated everything. Fantasy owners were at computer terminals, drafting teams. Professional football players walked around fully suited for the game. Stephen Jackson of the Rams. Phillip Rivers.

Aaron Rodgers. Maurice Jones-Drew. They were all walking around the room, keeping an eye on who was drafting them.

"I got you, Calvin," said a thick slob with glasses munching on a donut. He put up a tiny fist and fist-bumped Calvin Johnson of the Detroit Lions.

"Nice, Ian," said Calvin Johnson. "Now go get me a good quarterback."

"I'm on it, Megatron," muffled Ian through bites of his donut and then he coughed as he turned back to his draft board.

AP led Hairy through the dark draft room to the back. He opened large doors and a WHOOSH of air and bright light heightened their senses. As his eyes adjusted, Hairy saw that they were in fact inside of a domed NFL stadium.

On the artificial turf, several NFL players stretched and warmed up.

"Getting ready for Thursday Night Football," said AP.

Happy HairyBalls was in awe. "I had no idea fantasy football was so big," he said, watching the NFL players as they crisscrossed the field.

"Yeah, it's taken over," said Peterson. "Fans love all the action on Sundays. All in one place. The baseball season is too long, man. Too many games. You want action? You come here."

"Maybe the Director of the Baseball Writer's Association of America was right," said Hairy. "Maybe fantasy baseball can't compete with this."

Happy HairyBalls knew he had to get back to the others and tell them what he found, but he was oddly enchanted by the realm of fantasy football.

On the field, Drew Brees threw a deep bomb to Randy Moss streaking down the sideline.

Without breaking stride, Moss hauled in the 60-yard heave and ran to the End Zone.

"All Day, baby!" exclaimed Peterson. "All-Day!"

From across the field, a posse of NFL players approached, led by a familiar helmeted foe.

"Christian Batista," Happy HairyBalls said. "Didn't expect to see you here."

"Why not?" Batista's voice was muffled behind the face shield. "This is where the action is. And I am always near the action."

Hairy looked over the giant NFL players surrounding him.

"This is my fantasy football team, the S.B. Ballers," Batista said. "I have been sent here by Alvin the Hutt to recruit you into his Endless Summer Fantasy Football League. The entry fee is $200."

Hairy looked back but Adrain Peterson was gone. Vanished.

HairyBalls looked at the players warming up on the field. He could get quite a team for $200, he thought. And that was twice as much money to win.

"Can I still do fantasy baseball?" Hairy asked.

Batista laughed. "Sure, sure," he said. "You can be in as many fantasy leagues as you want. But why do you want to hang around those losers? Join us, and soon you'll wonder why you ever even bothered with fantasy baseball at all."

Batista flipped open a laptop for him. "Now, if you'll just log in here," he said.

"THERE HE IS!" From the tunnel, the man in the cheap suit pointed at Happy HairyBalls. An angry horde of mascots ran across the football field towards him.

Hairy quickly typed his information. He looked up at the charging mascots, some doing hand-springs and flips as they raced towards him. Hairy pressed ENTER.

His body dissolved, along with Batista and his fantasy team, disappearing into thin air.

The sun was bright and warm on his face. That was the first impression that struck Happy HairyBalls. The cool air tickled his cheeks. He shielded his eyes and squinted, trying to adjust to the bright sunlight. His boots scratched the dirt and small rock underneath. He stood up straight and looked out over the seemingly endless flat prairie, to the shaded mountains in the distance, and he took a long deep breath of mountain air.

"Wisconsin," he realized. "I'm home."

He walked along the dirt road, the rocks scratching under his boots.

He was all alone on the road for about a mile or so when he started to hear a sporadic whistle. As he got closer, he heard the grunts and yelps of youth. A high school football team was at practice on a big open field. The coach shouted instruction.

Beyond the practice field, Happy HairyBalls followed the road to a small town.

The buildings had a dusting of the Old West, the people a slow pace of contentment. The car traffic was light, and pickups stopped for crossing pedestrians. Happy HairyBalls walked up to a bus stop. There was an old man sitting on the bench reading a newspaper.

"Maa-an, gonna be a good one," said the old man behind the paper. "Opening Night. The Saints matchup against the Vikings. Brett Favre on the Vikings. Drew Brees and the Saints. Thursday Night Football. Gonna be a good one."

"I'm thinking of taking Adrian Peterson with my first pick," said HairyBalls.

The old man pulled down the paper. "You like the NFL?" he asked him.

Happy couldn't believe it. It was Walter Payton! Running back for the Bears!

"Uh, uh, yeah, yes," stammered Hairy. "Are you...?"

"You know it," said Walter Payton. "They call me Sweetness. My friend Ozzie told me you might be stopping by."

The bright sunlight twinkled in Walter Payton's eye.

"Come' on, I'll show you around the place," he said.

They walked off down the dusty rural street together and Happy HairyBalls was never seen in the fantasy baseball universe ever again.

It's Our Time, Down Here

The Matchup of the Century raged on. A baseball was ripped down the line, stabbed at third, and rocketed across the infield to beat the hard-charging runner. The crowd cheered, the crowd groaned, all were exasperated at the intensity of every moment as they hung onto the edge of their plastic stadium seats.

The sun was low in the sky, but the gentle pleasantness of the warm evening promised a wonderful night. The action on the field was quick, the close plays were remarkable, the sheer bizarreness of it had everyone captivated. Even though Satan's Bullpen had been behind the whole game, they kept clawing themselves off the mat, battling for every inch, and they stared down the behemoths of McGwire's All-Stars fearlessly.

Cali Green's back foot lifted high over his head on his follow-through as he spun in a slider. SMACK. Big Mac crushed it. He casually tossed the bat aside, his red helmet glistening in the lights, his puffy red eyes lifted to the upper deck where his ball was soaring. The whole stadium watched his towering home run as it rose up and up and over the McDonald's **BigMac LAND** sign and disappeared.

The scoreboard lit up another 8 points:

McGwire's All-Stars:	670
1. Brown Mosquitos:	438
4. SB Cherry Poppers:	415
2. Crazy Fool:	442
3. Mesa T's:	489

The Brown Mosquito had seen enough. He buzzed out of the dugout high up into the sky. He lifted over the crowd to the very top of the stadium and perched himself on the top wall.

High above the city he spotted ESPN Headquarters, the shoebox shaped compound with the satellite dish on the roof. He watched as the dish moved into position and the tractor beam hauled in another ship, easing it down in a purple glowing beam.

In the dugout, the mood was doom.

"We're never gonna beat these guys! It's over!" Crazy Fool slammed his glove down.

A fan behind the dugout eased a bucket on a rope down into the dugout. A white towel was draped over the side. The bucket read: SURRENDER SUPPLIES $1.00.

The players groaned. "Shut yar bloody traps and quit yar whining!" Captain Shitbeard was just as frustrated. "What did ya think was gonna happen?"

"I thought the famous Captain Shitbeard would finish better than 7-15," said Adam Horn. "Have you been asleep the whole second half of the season?"

"Flism Flasm Da," said the Captain. "I've been paying no attention to this league for three months now! I have guys on the DL in my starting lineup! Three of 'em!"

"Actually, four if you count your relief pitcher whose been out since May," said TJ.

"This league was doomed from the start," moaned Crazy Fool.

The Mosquito buzzed back in. "I have some more bad news. It looks like Happy HairyBalls wasn't able to shut off the tractor beam." All the players groaned.

"Well, that makes it official. The season's over, boys," said Adam Horn. "Anyone going to the fantasy football galaxy?"

"Didn't you hear what he said?" shouted Crazy Fool. "No one's leaving here. We'll die in this fantasy baseball universe. Never to be heard from again."

"Well, then," said Captain Shitbeard. "If we're gonna be sitting around like old women, I'd rather sit around with a drink in my hand. Let's go, Cali Green."

The rest of them followed down the steps to the locker room tunnel, dejected.

"Wait," TJ said. "You can't go."

Cali kicked his long blonde locks down the back of his neck and slipped on his round green shades. "Yeah? Why is that?" he asked.

TJ looked at his feet, unable to respond.

"Because there are two teams left for the 2009 Championship," said Adam Horn.

Captain Shitbeard stopped at the base of the stairs and turned to hear.

"Mesa T's will face the Brown Mosquitos for the title," said Horn.

Everyone in the dugout looked over the two final competitors, hardened with the grind of the regular season and first-round victories.

"Well, good luck," said Shitbeard. "I'll ring the bell and toast the winner."

"Don't you see? Look how far we've come!" shouted TJ. "We gotta chance!"

SF Tranny on Crak picked up her cue.

"A chance at what?" Tranny asked, teary-eyed. "Getting killed? Look, if we keep going someone's really gonna get hurt, maybe dead."

Heads nodded.

TJ's puppy dog eyes pleaded with them. "But if you leave, what then? We'll all just go back to our lives as bartenders, and students, and audio/video salesmen, and pharmacists, and bar-backs who get their tips in an envelope filled with ketchup."

The slow gentle waves of music carried on the breeze, an uplifting cinematic melody that would inspire even the most faint of spirit.

"Don't you realize?" TJ shouted. "The next time you see the sky, it'll be over another town. The next time you take a test, it'll be in some other school. Our parents. They want the best of stuff for us, but right now they gotta do what's right for them, 'cause it's their time, their time! Up there. Down here, it's our time. It's our time, down here. That's all over the second we ride up Big Mac's bucket."

He slapped the SURRENDER bucket with the white towel.

They looked each other in the eyes, understanding the importance of this moment. And they realized that they were nothing more than Goonies themselves, right in the middle of an adventure of their own. The music rose to a crescendo and then suddenly stopped. A rising theater-like applause from the Busch Stadium crowd ensued.

SF Tranny had tears in her eyes as she stared proudly at TJ. Her eye black started to run down her cheeks.

The fans rose to their feet, shouting and clapping.

SF Tranny cried, and clasped her hands together. "This was what I always wanted," she said. "To hear the applause."

The loudspeaker boomed, "Ladies and Gentlemen, that was TJ and the San Francisco Tranny on Crak, performing the scene from Goonies: 'It's Our Time, Down Here,' produced by the San Francisco Tranny on Crak."

The fans cheered and showered the ball-field with roses.

Crazy Fool took SF Tranny by the arm and led her out of the dugout to the roar of the crowd.

"We did it, Crazy Fool," she said.

"You did it," he said and took a step back.

SF Tranny took an elaborate bow and blew kisses to the adoring crowd. The fans continued to throw red roses.

The Brown Mosquito listened to the crowd. Suddenly a plan dawned. Barry Bonds made his way to the plate. "Hey Horn," the Mosquito asked as he watched Bonds warm up. "How many points for a walk?"

"A walk? One," Horn replied. "The pitcher gets negative one."

"Right, negative one," said the Mosquito. "And how many negative points for a hit batter?" he asked.

"Zero," Horn said and smiled. He looked at Cali.

Cali Green shrugged. "I'm down for whatever, man," he said.

The crowd cheered as Barry Bonds came to the plate. The little girl in the stands turned to her grandpa. "That's Barry Bonds, grandpa," she said proudly. "He hit 73 home runs in a season. That's an all-time record."

"I know, I remember," said the grandpa. "We used to have a fella by the name of Roger Maris who held that record. He passed the legendary Babe Ruth with 61 home runs in a season. That record stood for a long time. But between 1998 and 2001, that record was broken 6 times by 3 men! Can you believe it? Sammy Sosa broke the record 3 times in those 3 years! And McGwire had two seasons that each shattered the old record – until Barry Bonds hit the most of all with 73!"

"Don't you think that's strange?" the girl asked. "After all those years, those 3 men broke all those records again and again and again?"

"Yes, I do. In fact, between you and me, I really believe Roger Maris still holds that record," said the grandpa. "And Babe Ruth is number two. Someday they'll set the record straight."

On the mound, Cali Green looked in for the sign. SF Tranny nodded. The Mosquito pounded his glove, Carlos Correa right beside him.

Barry Bonds growled like a junk yard dog.

Cali Green kicked and delivered a blazing fastball right at Bonds that hit him just above his massive elbow gear.

Bonds winced and growled. He rubbed his shoulder and snarled at Cali Green.

Cali Green took the ball back from the ump and started whistling on his way back up to the mound.

The next batter was Alex Rodriguez. Cali Green nodded to SF Tranny. He kicked and delivered — a BLAZING FASTBALL just over the head of A-Rod that SLAMMED HARD into the backstop.

Barry jogged up to second base on the wild pitch as SF Tranny retrieved the ball.

“See what happens if you do that again,” A-Rod spit dip juice and pointed his bat at Cali Green.

“Time,” SF Tranny held her hands up, and propped the catcher's mask upon her head.

“TIME!” shouted the ump.

“Are there negative points for a passed ball or wild pitch?” she asked him.

“Zero,” shouted the ump.

“Ok, we’re good then,” SF Tranny smiled and flipped the mask back down. “Here we go, Cali.”

She flipped her finger down under his/her crotch and wiggled it. Then pointed it inside. Way inside.

Cali Green nodded. He went into his windup, and fired a fastball that SMACKED INTO A-ROD’S HELMET — SHATTERING IT!

Stunned, A-Rod wobbled back.

“HEY!” shouted Benito Santiago from the dugout. “Es me amigo puto bendehoe!”

McGwire’s team poured out of the dugout, charging with rage-induced blood vessels nearly popping out of their skulls. They ROARED like gorillas.

The Rocket Roger Clemens got to the mound first and cocked his arm back to unload on Cali Green but he was CRACKED across the jaw by the heavy fist of Captain Shitbeard!

Adam Horn was bombarded by both Giambi brothers. He fought them off by dodging punches and throwing explosive counter-punches.

The Mosquito bzzzzzzz'd and bzzzzzzzzzzzzz'd and bZZZZZzzzzzzzZZZZZZzzzzzzzzz'd all over the place, stinging both Ken Caminiti and then Sammy Sosa.

Crazy Fool went ape-shit, taking out mother-fuckas with rock hard fists. He knocked out Manny Ramirez, then kicked him down, jumped over him and pounded Andy Pettitte square in the nose.

Someone grabbed the Newport Idiot's thin lingerie uniform and ripped it, exposing the Idiot's hairy chest.

The crowd couldn't believe it. A full-on bench-clearing brawl between Satan's Bullpen and the superstar athletes.

With an iron fist, Mark McGwire clubbed the Newport Idiot. He turned to SF Tranny and took him/her out with a three-punch combo. Then something suddenly caught his eye. The scoreboard. The Brown Mosquito score was rising, and so was Mesa T's.

McGwire's team score hadn't moved from 670.

As the fight raged on in the infield, the hologram players of Mesa T's continued to play the game against the hologram players of the Brown Mosquitos.

Wearing the White, Red, and Blue of the Mesa T's, Victor Martinez clubbed a home run, his 23rd of the season. Next up, Evan Longoria hit his 33rd to go along with 113 RBI.

Andre Either and Adam Lind joined the party, smashing balls over the fence, and Michael Bourn dazzled with 61 stolen bases.

The Mosquitos fought back with everything they had. Ricky Nolasco and A.J. Burnett powered the attack with 195 Strikeouts each. Chad Billingsley added 179, Jared Weaver had 174, and Ubaldo Jimenez topped them all with 198 K's for the season.

Justin Verlander reared back and fired a strike to Chase Utley of the Mosquitos.

"STRRRRRRRRIKE THREE!" the ump punched his fist.

Two points were added to the **Mesa T's** for the strikeout. A point was subtracted from the **Brown Mosquitos.** The score of **McGwire's All-Stars** remained the same.

McGwire growled in anger at the scoreboard. He stomped off back toward the dugout.

Amid the chaos, the Brown Mosquito saw him go. He boxed Benito Santiago's balls like a speed bag, his 6 hard fists a blur of punishment. Santiago keeled over and crumbled. The Brown Mosquito buzzed off under thrusting kicks and powerful punches to follow McGwire, heading into the dugout and down the tunnel.

The tunnel went on and on under the stadium with the showers and offices and weight rooms and press rooms and on and on. The Brown Mosquito turned a corner and caught a glimpse of Cardinal red disappearing down the far end.

The Brown Mosquito bzzzzzzzzzzzz'd after him, like the miniature fighter jet he was, his needle-tipped nose piercing through the air. The tunnels continued on and on. He soon realized they were beyond the bowels of the stadium. There were exits to the city above, marked with street and avenue names, a subterranean maze leading him further downtown.

The Mosquito heard a door close up ahead and turned a corner.

When he finally reached the door it read:

ESPN Headquarters.
Authorized Personnel Only.

The door was locked, but the Brown Mosquito wiggled underneath. He ascended the stairs, and found himself in the large airplane hanger-like room. The click and clack of skateboards was everywhere. ESPN X-Games athletes were practicing on the several connecting halfpipes throughout the chamber. Extreme athletes launched into the air, holding their board as they spun and flipped, incredibly turning their wheels back to the ramp at the last possible instance to ride to the other side of the halfpipe and launch again.

The Mosquito looked up and saw Big Mac hurry along a gangplank to the other side of the room. He disappeared through a heavy metal door. The Mosquito buzzed across the room but was met with flying bogeys from all directions. The Mosquito dodged the skateboards with radical maneuvers of his own. Halfway across there was a huge halfpipe, and before he could react, an unseen boarder shot off the lip and the Brown Mosquito was caught in his jet-stream.

It drafted him higher and higher and spun him as the athlete went into a 720 McTwist. Dazed and dizzy at the apex of the launch, the Mosquito was suddenly pulled back as the skateboard blazed back down to the ramp. The board landed with the Mosquito flying right with it. They rode down the ramp, and then rocketed up off the other end. The Mosquito shot up into the air and crashed onto the gangplank.

Shaking off his dizziness, the Mosquito fluttered up to the door. It was locked, and there was no room to sneak in underneath. There were reinforced windows into the next room, and the Brown Mosquito put his face up against them. He looked in and saw all the huge glass vials of bubbling brown liquid. High above was the octagon-shaped glass ceiling and the satellite dish on the roof.

The Mosquito entered the room through a vent, right over Big Mac, furiously typing at a bank of computers.

"I've got to get some stats pumped in there before it's too late!" he said to himself as he increased Home Runs for Jeremy Giambi, Manny Ramirez, and Alex Rodriguez.

Through the glass panels on the ceiling, the satellite was triggered and illuminated a purple beam across the sky.

"Ahhhhhh!" McGwire shouted in surprise as a sting pierced his ginger skin.

Behind him was the Brown Mosquito with a drop of blood hanging from his nose.

McGwire turned beat red.

"Give it up, Big Mac," said the Mosquito. "Your time is done. I'm taking control of this league."

"Never!" McGwire swung his bat at him, and the Mosquito ducked out of the way just in time. McGwire swung and missed again, waving his baseball bat after the pesky Mosquito. It waved with a "whoom."

The Mosquito landed on the computer keyboard. McGwire ROARED and swung his bat down, SMASHING it into the computer. Red and yellow sparks flew, sending the Mosquito crashing into a monitor.

McGwire's baseball bat electrified with the sparks from the computer and started to glow red bolts throughout the wood. He was mesmerized as he held the bat with his massive forearms.

Sitting in the blue haze of the broken monitor, the Brown Mosquito was electrified as well, blue bolts darting through his body and making his needle nose glow.

McGwire turned and swung the glowing red bat with a "whoomp."

The bat was met head-on in a CLASH OF SPARKS by the GLOWING BLUE STINGER of the Brown Mosquito!

McGwire wielded his bat around again with a whoom and again it collided with the glowing blue stinger! A storm of sparks lit up the room as the swords collided again and again. The Mosquito fought him back, crashing his stinger over and over into McGwire's bat.

"You can't defeat me! I am too powerful!" McGwire shouted and came at him with hard thrusts, parried desperately by the little blue stinger. Big Mac backed the

Mosquito to the edge of the platform, high above the cavern of glass vials hanging by thick cables.

The Brown Mosquito tried to hold his balance, backed to the very edge. But before he got his footing, another strike was upon him, and he was swatted over the brink.

The Mosquito fell, far down into the abyss.

McGwire lost sight of him between all the glass vials of the brown bubbling juice.

"Ha," he laughed. "Exterminated."

McGwire returned to the computer, a smashed mess of sparks and broken screens. He was pissed. "I need to get those juiced stats to the players. I'm running out of time!"

The computer was unusable. He looked up at the glass ceiling and the satellite dish and knew what he had to do.

Strong gusts of wind whipped violently on the roof of the ESPN building, and pulled through McGwire's short red curls on the top of his head. His massive biceps and forearms strained with tension as he tried to physically turn the very large and heavy satellite dish. He pulled and pulled, forcing the dish and it's purple beam towards his target, Busch Stadium, off in the distance.

The purple ray flickered and McGwire used all his strength to heave it into position. The spotlight got closer and closer as it crept across the city toward the ballpark and the cheering crowd.

Inside the ballpark, the infield and outfield was a scene of carnage, like after a battle in Game of Thrones or Braveheart. Painful groans and desperate pleas of players dragging themselves across the dirt. Captain Shitbeard leaned against the leg of Jason Giambi, his face bruised and bloody from several gashes on his cheeks and forehead. He popped off a cork with his teeth and spit it out. He greedily chugged the whiskey, and then took a dying breath.

Cali Green was face-down in the grass, beaten and bloody. SF Tranny was sprawled over the back of Crazy Fool, barely breathing. Adam Horn crawled on his elbows to the Newport Idiot, his legs badly damaged.

"You... you okay, buddy?" He finally reached the Idiot and shook his shoulder.

"War," was all the Idiot could manage.

"I know, buddy," said Horn. "I know. Well, it looks like this is it."

"Waaar," he said.

"I know, buddy," said Horn. "Me, too."

A couple of McGwire's All-Stars were surveying the carnage, kicking bodies. They looked up as a purple glow illuminated the sky.

On the roof of ESPN, Big Mac concluded pulling the dish into position. "Now to infuse a little juice into this game," he started to say, but suddenly stopped.

In the wind, he thought he heard something. A far off sound. Something small, yet very large. Quiet, yet ominous. An uncomfortable hum that was getting closer and its pitch was rising. Big Mac soon realized it wasn't coming from a single source, but from many, many sources. The same high frequency, produced from hundreds or even thousands of something very tiny.

And then they were upon him. HUNDREDS OF THOUSANDS OF BROWN MOSQUITOS SWARMED!

The buzzing was overwhelming. McGwire put his hands to his face as they attacked him. He swatted and flailed and screamed to no avail. He stumbled backward, swinging his arms.

The Brown Mosquito bzzzzzzzzzzzz'd his needled nose right into Big Mac's fat neck and drew an ounce of blood. McGwire clasped his neck and a large welt grew and grew on it. He stumbled back.

The Mosquito drank the blood, satisfied. But then he tasted something that surprised him.

His eyes bugged out when he realized… "Dad?" he asked, stunned.

"Son..." was all McGwire managed to say as his giant body CRASHED backward through the glass ceiling. His arms reached out as he plummeted, crashing through the large glass vials of bubbling brown liquid on his way down.

The ceiling collapsed and the satellite dish plunged after him, into the huge vials as they all exploded in shattered glass. The brown liquid flooded the room.

The Brown Mosquito looked down from above, watching the man who spawned him disappear to his death.

At the stadium, the purple light flickered off. Horn looked up, "The tractor beam," he said. "He did it."

Brown Mosquito hurler Chad Billingsley fired a pitch.

TJ swung and connected, driving the ball deep.

José Canseco went back, and back, and back to the wall…

The ball bounced off the top of Canseco's head and popped over the wall!

A HOME RUN!

TJ thrust his arms in victory! The crowd went crazy!

Canseco rubbed his head and looked over the wall, wondering what just happened.

TJ ran the bases, elated. Cameras flashed. He waved to the fans. The scoreboard numbers twitched and twinkled and flashed and finally came to rest to read:

FINAL SCORE:

Mesa T'S:	826
Brown Mosquitos:	710
McGwire's All-Stars:	0.0

"He did it," said Crazy Fool. "The stats. They're gone." The scoreboard flickered and then displayed:

ALL-TIME HOME RUN LEADERS:

1. Hank Aaron	755
2. Babe Ruth	714
3. Willie Mays	660

Captain Shitbeard looked up with his one good eye.

"He did it," said SF Tranny, looking up at the numbers.

MOST HOME RUNS IN A SEASON:

1. Roger Maris	61
2. Babe Ruth	60
3. Babe Ruth	59

"He did it," said the grandpa, standing up out of his seat with his granddaughter.

Fireworks detonated in the sky and continued throughout the night, explosions from McGwire's steroid lab at ESPN Headquarters.

TJ rounded third, his short chubby legs barely touching the ground, pumping his fist over and over.

The crowd stood and cheered. The scoreboard read:

2009 Champion: MESA T'S

The rest of the crew was waiting for him at home plate and cheered him on.

TJ STOMPED ON HOME PLATE.

Captain Shitbeard picked him up and lifted him into the air, holding him high over his head. The others reached up and carried TJ, waving to the fans as the fireworks lit up the sky.

*NOTE: This final play of the inaugural season was captured on film and can be seen by going to youtube and searching: "Jose Canseco Ball Hits Head."

Field of Dreams

The sun was bright and the air was warm. A soft breeze ruffled the leaves of corn stalks. The Brown Mosquito pulled on his dusty old Brown Mosquito cap and headed out into the field. First, he checked the vegetable garden. Tomatoes were big and green. Won't be long now. Summer was right around the corner. He went to the coop and fed the chickens. It was a gorgeous morning. The sun felt good through his long sleeves.

The dogs followed him across the yard as he walked to the cornfield. Growing taller, he thought. He bent down and noticed the soil was moist from the drip lines. The dogs started barking.

The Brown Mosquito adjusted his hat and took a lasting look into the corn stalks.

"Come' on, guys," he said to the dogs.

He led the dogs to his barn and workshop. He went right to his workbench and picked up a wood carving, shaped somewhat like a small bedpost.

The Brown Mosquito picked it up in his hand, felt the weight, the feeling of it as he spun it lightly around. He took a piece of well-worn sandpaper and smoothed a few spots. He pulled down the paint. Three cans; black, blue, and orange.

"Time for school!" he heard his wife shout from inside the house.

At the kitchen door, the Brown Mosquito gave Brother Mosquito and Sister Mosquito hugs and kisses and slapped their backpacks on their way out the door. The kids ran to the corner where the school bus was waiting for them.

He wrapped his arm around Mama Mosquito and they waved.

Finished, painted, and dried, the carving rested gently in the Mosquito's hand as he walked out into the cornfield. The dogs barked but stopped at the edge of the corn, then went back to sniffing around the yard.

The Mosquito continued on, waving the leaves of the stalks out of the way.

"Hey, Brown Mosquito," a ball-player joined him, also walking through the stalks.

"Hey, Timmy," he said to Tim Lincecum, pitcher for the San Francisco Giants, but wearing the Green, Blue, and Silver of the Cali Green uniform. "You have a good looking squad over there this year."

"Yeah, you, too, man," said Timmy.

"Sorry we didn't draft you this year, Timmy," said the Mosquito. "You went too high. Number 2 overall! Congratulations."

"Ah, thanks, man. You guys have some talent on your team. Maybe a chance to win it this year," said Lincecum.

"Hope so," said the Mosquito. "That's the plan."

The Brown Mosquito couldn't help but smile. As Timmy disappeared into the corn, the 2010 Brown Mosquitos filed in around him, walking through the stalks with him. Carl Crawford. Robinson Cano. Miguel Cabrera. Johan Santana. Matt Cain. Cole Hamels. A.J. Burnett. Jered Weaver. Billy Wagner. All wearing the brown and yellow.

The light got brighter as a clearing was ahead. The Brown Mosquito looked down at the carving he held in his hand.

Miraculously it now held a figure at the end. A bobbled-headed ballplayer.

The Brown Mosquito gently rocked it in his hand and the Tim Lincecum bobblehead wobbled back and forth, the headpiece of the trophy.

On the bedpost-shaped base of the trophy there was a plaque commemorating the League Champion:

2009
MESA T'S
Taylor Jordan

The corn stalks opened up into the outfield of a baseball stadium. The crowd CHEERED as the Brown Mosquitos took the field in their home whites. The players started tossing the ball around and warming up. The Brown Mosquito made his way to the pitching mound where the others were waiting for him.

"Hey! Let's get this thing started! I don't have all day!" shouted Captain Shitbeard. He passed around a Jaegermeister bottle. "But first, a drink!" he shouted, "To TJ!"

They all clapped and some of them rubbed TJ's head. TJ blushed and smiled.

"To the winner of the Championship," the Brown Mosquito announced, "goes the $500 Championship prize – plus the other teams' late fees – and your name forever immortalized on the Satan's Bullpen Championship trophy; The Timmy!"

The Mosquito held up the trophy with the bobble-headed Tim Lincecum poised on one leg, head bobbling. He handed it to TJ, who took it very delicately in two hands. Then he thrust the trophy high into the sky, and the Timmy bobbled as the crowd cheered.

"Good Luck this year, gentlemen," said the Brown Mosquito. "May the best man..." he stopped suddenly. Saw a face he didn't recognize.

"Who are you?" the Brown Mosquito asked.

The large-headed man turned his fat jowls towards the Brown Mosquito. "I am Alvin," he boomed. "I will be playing under the team name Alvin's Romans."

"Alvin the Hutt," said the Brown Mosquito.

Christian Batista stood beside him, his helmeted mask pulled down.

"Batista," said Adam Horn. "I should've known."

"Well, as long as everyone's paid," said the Brown Mosquito. "And if you haven't, it goes up $10 a month until you do. Late fees will go to the eventual Champion." The Brown Mosquito continued, going once again over the rules and playoff situation, the payouts and free agency system. The nine others listened intently as the outfielders and infielders whipped the ball around. The starting pitcher was getting ready in the bullpen.

"*And it's a beautiful day for baseball*," the TV announcer began the broadcast. "The Brown Mosquitos take on Captain Shitbeard in what should promise to be a highly competitive opening week match-up."

Through the TV screen, we are in the Brown Mosquito's living room. He sits comfortably on his couch with a large Sapphire Gimlet on the rocks in his hand, watching the game. His kids run circles around him. Every once in awhile one of them belly flops on top of him and he has to tickle them off of him to see the game. The first pitch is fired in for a strike. A new season has begun.

NOT THE END

Satan's Bullpen Champions

2009 Mesa T's – Taylor Jordan
2010 Captain Shitbeard – Mike Holland
2011 Brown Mosquitos – Adam Anton
2012 Brown Mosquitos – Adam Anton
2013 Tijuana Thyne Bombers – Taylor Jordan
2014 Buellton Beaver Beaters – Chris Smith
2015 Brown Mosquitos – Adam Anton
2016 California Trout Ticklers – Ryan Bouton
2017 Brown Mosquitos – Adam Anton
2018 Hallucinating Hummingbirds – Sean Lappi
2019 Buellton Beaver Beaters – Chris Smith

The Timmy

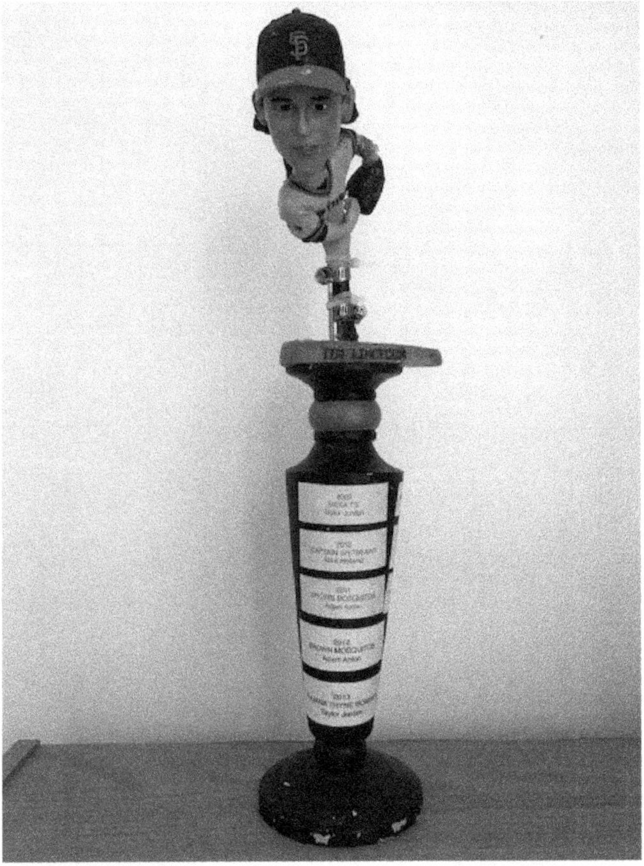